In my formative years as a young C
the fact that I faced many challeng
behaviour. Few writers helped me
respond to these challenges and think ... ... Christian as much
as John Stott did. The challenges of faithfulness to God's way are
more acute and complex today than when I was a young Christian.
In these little books, you find the essence of Stott's thinking about
the Christian life; it is refreshing to read this material again and see
how relevant and health-giving it is for today. I'm grateful to Inter-
Varsity Press and to Tim Chester for making Stott's thinking
accessible to a new generation.

Ajith Fernando, Teaching Director, Youth for Christ, Sri Lanka

Technology has enabled more voices to clamour for our attention
than ever before, while, at the same time, people's ability to listen
carefully seems to have deteriorated as never before. John Stott's
speaking and writing was renowned for two things in particular: he
taught us how to listen attentively to God in order to live faithfully
for God; and he modelled how to listen to the world sensitively in
order to communicate God's purposes intelligibly. He taught us to
listen. That is why it is such a thrill to see *The Contemporary Christian*
carefully revived in a new format as a series for a new generation of
readers. As we read, may we listen well!

Mark Meynell, Director (Europe and Caribbean) Langham
Preaching, Langham Partnership and author of *Cross-Examined*
and *When Darkness Seems My Closest Friend*

It is always refreshing, enlightening and challenging reading from
the pen of John Stott. I am totally delighted that one of his most
significant works will continue to be available, hopefully for more
decades to come. The way Stott strives to be faithful to the Word of
God and relevant to his world – secularized Western society – as the
locus for the drama of God's action, is exemplary, especially for those

of us ordained to the service of the church in our diverse contexts. I highly commend The Contemporary Christian series to all who share the same pursuit – listening intently to God's Word and God's world, hearing and obeying God.

David Zac Niringiye, author of *The Church: God's Pilgrim People*

I am delighted that a new generation will now be able to benefit from this rich teaching, which so helped me when it first appeared. As always with John Stott, there is a wonderful blend of faithful exposition of the Bible, rigorous engagement with the world and challenging applications for our lives.

Vaughan Roberts, Rector, St Ebbe's Church, Oxford, and author of a number of books, including *God's Big Picture* (IVP)

Imagine being like a child overwhelmed by hundreds of jigsaw puzzle pieces – you just can't put them together! And then imagine that a kindly old uncle comes along and helps you to assemble the whole thing, piece by piece. That is what it felt like reading John Stott's book *The Contemporary Christian*. For those of us who feel we can't get our heads around our Bibles, let alone our world, he comes along and, with his staggering gifts of clarity and insight, helps us, step by step, to work out what it means to understand our world through biblical lenses. It's then a great blessing to have Tim Chester's questions at the end of each chapter, which help us to think through and internalize each step.

Rico Tice, Senior Minister for Evangelism, All Souls, Langham Place, London, and co-author of *Christianity Explored*

I have long benefited from the work of John Stott because of the way he combines rigorous engagement of the biblical text and careful engagement with the culture of his day. The Contemporary Christian series presents Stott at his very best. It displays his commitment to biblical authority, his zeal for the mission of the church and his call to faithful witness in the world. Stott's reflections here are a must-read for church leaders today.

Trevin Wax, Director of Bibles and Reference, LifeWay Christian Resources, and author of *This Is Our Time* and *Eschatological Discipleship*

All the royalties from this book have been irrevocably assigned to Langham Literature. Langham Literature is a ministry of Langham Partnership, founded by John Stott. Chris Wright is the International Ministries Director.

Langham Literature provides Majority World preachers, scholars and seminary libraries with evangelical books and electronic resources through publishing and distribution, grants and discounts. They also foster the creation of indigenous evangelical books in many languages through writers' grants, strengthening local evangelical publishing houses and investment in major regional literature projects.

For further information on Langham Literature, and the rest of Langham Partnership, visit the website at <www.langham.org>.

The Contemporary Christian

THE CHURCH

A Unique Gathering of People

John Stott with Tim Chester

INTER-VARSITY PRESS
36 Causton Street, London SW1P 4ST, England
Email: ivp@ivpbooks.com
Website: www.ivpbooks.com

This volume has been adapted from John Stott, *The Contemporary Christian* (1992), and is one of five titles published in this format in The Contemporary Christian series, with extra text, including questions, by Tim Chester.

British Library Cataloguing-in-Publication Data
A catalogue record for this book is available from the British Library.

ISBN: 978–1–78359–924–0
eBook ISBN: 978–1–78359–925–7

Set in Minion

Typeset in Great Britain by CRB Associates, Potterhanworth, Lincolnshire
Print and production managed in Great Britain by Jellyfish Print Solutions

Inter-Varsity Press publishes Christian books that are true to the Bible and that communicate the gospel, develop discipleship and strengthen the church for its mission in the world.

IVP originated within the Inter-Varsity Fellowship, now the Universities and Colleges Christian Fellowship, a student movement connecting Christian Unions in universities and colleges throughout Great Britain, and a member movement of the International Fellowship of Evangelical Students. Website: www.uccf.org.uk. That historic association is maintained, and all senior IVP staff and committee members subscribe to the UCCF Basis of Faith.

Contents

About the authors   viii

Preface   ix

A note to the reader   xi

Series introduction: the Contemporary Christian –
     the then and the now   1

The Church: introduction   9

   1   Secular challenges to the church   11

   2   Evangelism through the local church   25

   3   Dimensions of church renewal   42

   4   The church's pastors   55

Conclusion: the now and the not yet   72

Notes   82

About the authors

John Stott had a worldwide ministry as a church leader, a Bible expositor and the author of many award-winning books. He was Rector Emeritus of All Souls, Langham Place, London, and Founder-President of the Langham Partnership.

Tim Chester is Pastor of Grace Church, Boroughbridge, North Yorkshire, Chair of Keswick Ministries and the author of more than forty books.

Preface

To be 'contemporary' is to live in the present, and to move with the times without worrying too much about the past or the future.

To be a 'contemporary Christian', however, is to live in a present which is enriched by our knowledge of the past and by our expectation of the future. Our Christian faith demands this. Why? Because the God we trust and worship is 'the Alpha and the Omega . . . who is, and who was, and who is to come, the Almighty',[1] while the Jesus Christ we follow is 'the same yesterday and today and for ever'.[2]

So this book and series are about how Christians handle time – how we can bring the past, the present and the future together in our thinking and living. Two main challenges face us. The first is the tension between the 'then' (past) and the 'now' (present), and the second the tension between the 'now' (present) and the 'not yet' (future).

The Introduction opens up the first problem. Is it possible for us truly to honour the past and live in the present at the same time? Can we preserve Christianity's historic identity intact without cutting ourselves off from those around us? Can we communicate the gospel in ways that are exciting and modern without distorting or even destroying it? Can we be authentic and fresh at the same time, or do we have to choose?

The Conclusion opens up the second problem: the tension between the 'now' and the 'not yet'. How far can we explore and experience everything that God has said and done through Christ without straying into what has not yet been revealed or given? How can we develop a proper sense of humility about a future yet to unfold without becoming complacent about where we are in the present?

In between these enquiries into the influences of the past and the future comes an exploration about our Christian responsibilities in the present.

Preface

This series is about questions of doctrine and discipleship under the five headings: 'The Gospel', 'The Disciple', 'The Bible', 'The Church' (the book you are holding in your hands) and 'The World', though I make no attempt to be systematic, let alone exhaustive.

In addition to the topic of time, and the relations between past, present and future, there is a second theme running through this series: the need for us to talk less and listen more.

I believe we are called to the difficult and even painful task of 'double listening'. We are to listen carefully (although of course with differing degrees of respect) both to the ancient Word and to the modern world, in order to relate the one to the other with a combination of faithfulness and sensitivity.

Each book in this series is an attempt at double listening. It is my firm conviction that if we can only develop our capacity for double listening, we will avoid the opposite pitfalls of unfaithfulness and irrelevance, and truly be able to speak God's Word to God's world with effectiveness today.

Adapted from the original Preface by John Stott in 1991

A note to the reader

The original book entitled *The Contemporary Christian*, on which this volume and series are based, may not seem 'contemporary' to readers more than a quarter of a century later. But both the publisher and John Stott's Literary Executors are convinced that the issues which John Stott addresses in this book are every bit as relevant today as when they were first written.

The question was how to make this seminal work accessible for new generations of readers. We have sought to do this in the following ways:

- The original work has been divided into a series of several smaller volumes based on the five major sections of the original.
- Words that may not resonate with the twenty-first-century reader have been updated, while great care has been taken to maintain the thought process and style of the author in the original.
- Each chapter is now followed by questions from a current bestselling Christian author to aid reflection and response.

Lovers of the original work have expressed delight that this book is being made available in a way that extends its reach and influence well into a new century. We pray that your life will be enriched as you read, as the lives of many have already been greatly enriched by the original edition.

Series introduction
The Contemporary Christian –
the then and the now

The expression 'the contemporary Christian' strikes many as a contradiction in terms. Isn't Christianity an antique relic from the remote past, irrelevant to people in today's world?

My purpose in this series is to show that there is such a thing as 'contemporary Christianity' – not something newfangled, but original, historic, orthodox, biblical Christianity, sensitively related to the modern world.

Christianity: both historical and contemporary

We begin by reaffirming that Christianity is a historical religion. Of course, every religion arose in a particular historical context. Christianity, however, makes an especially strong claim to be historical because it rests not only on a historical *person*, Jesus of Nazareth, but on certain historical *events* which involved him, especially his birth, death and resurrection. There is a common thread here with the Judaism from which Christianity sprang. The Old Testament presents God not only as 'the God of Abraham, Isaac and Jacob', but also as the God of the covenant which he made with Abraham, and then renewed with Isaac and Jacob. Again, he is not only 'the God of Moses', but is also seen as the Redeemer responsible for the exodus, who went on to renew the covenant yet again at Mount Sinai.

Christians are forever tethered in heart and mind to these decisive, historical events of the past. We are constantly encouraged in the

Bible to look back to them with thankfulness. Indeed, God deliberately made provision for his people to recall his saving actions on a regular basis. Supremely, the Lord's Supper or Holy Communion enables us to call the atoning death of Christ regularly to mind, and so bring the past into the present.

But the problem is that Christianity's foundational events took place such a long time ago. I had a conversation with two brothers some years ago – students who told me they had turned away from the faith of their parents. One was now an agnostic, the other an atheist. I asked why. Did they no longer believe in the truth of Christianity? No, their dilemma was not whether Christianity was *true*, but whether it was *relevant*. How could it be? Christianity, they went on, was a primitive, Palestinian religion from long ago. So what on earth did it have to offer them, living in the exciting modern world?

This view of Christianity is widespread. The world has changed dramatically since Jesus' day, and goes on changing with ever more bewildering speed. People reject the gospel, not necessarily because they think it false, but because it no longer resonates with them.

In response to this we need to be clear about the basic Christian conviction that God continues to speak through what he has spoken. His Word is not a prehistoric fossil, but a living message for the contemporary world. Even granted the historical particularities of the Bible and the immense complexities of the modern world, there is still a fundamental correspondence between them. God's Word remains a lamp to our feet and a light for our path.[1]

At the same time, our dilemma remains. Can Christianity both retain its authentic identity *and* demonstrate its relevance?

The desire to present Jesus in a way that appeals to our own generation is obviously right. This was the preoccupation of the German pastor Dietrich Bonhoeffer while in prison during World War 2: 'What is bothering me incessantly,' he wrote, 'is the question . . . who

Christ really is for us today?'² It is a difficult question. In answering it, the church has tended in every generation to develop images of Christ which deviate from the portrait painted by the New Testament authors.

Attempting to modernize Jesus

Here are some of the church's many attempts to present a contemporary picture of Christ, some of which have been more successful than others in remaining loyal to the original.

I think first of *Jesus the ascetic* who inspired generations of monks and hermits. He was much like John the Baptist, for he too dressed in a camel's hair cloak, wore sandals or went barefoot, and munched locusts with evident relish. But it would be hard to reconcile this portrait with his contemporaries' criticism that he was a party-goer who 'came eating and drinking'.³

Then there was *Jesus the pale Galilean*. The apostate emperor Julian tried to reinstate Rome's pagan gods after Constantine had replaced them with the worship of Christ, and is reported as having said on his deathbed in AD 363, 'You have conquered, O Galilean.' His words were popularized by the nineteenth-century poet Swinburne:

Thou hast conquered, O pale Galilean;
The world has grown grey from thy breath.

This image of Jesus was perpetuated in medieval art and stained glass, with a heavenly halo and a colourless complexion, eyes lifted to the sky and feet never quite touching the ground.

In contrast to the presentations of Jesus as weak, suffering and defeated, there was *Jesus the cosmic Christ*, much loved by the Byzantine church leaders. They depicted him as the King of kings and Lord of lords, the creator and ruler of the universe. Yet, exalted high above all things, glorified and reigning, he seemed aloof from

3

the real world, and even from his own humanity, as revealed in the incarnation and the cross.

At the opposite end of the theological spectrum, the seventeenth- and eighteenth-century deists of the Enlightenment constructed in their own image *Jesus the teacher of common sense*,[4] entirely human and not divine at all. The most dramatic example is the work of Thomas Jefferson, President of the United States from 1801 to 1809. Rejecting the supernatural as incompatible with reason, he produced his own edition of the Gospels, in which all miracles and mysteries were systematically eliminated. What is left is a guide to a merely human moral teacher.

In the twentieth century we were presented with a wide range of options. Two of the best known owe their popularity to musicals. There is *Jesus the clown* of *Godspell*, who spends his time singing and dancing, and thus captures something of the gaiety of Jesus, but hardly takes his mission seriously. Somewhat similar is *Jesus Christ Superstar*, the disillusioned celebrity who once thought he knew who he was, but in Gethsemane was no longer sure.

The late President of Cuba, Fidel Castro, frequently referred to Jesus as 'a great revolutionary', and there have been many attempts to portray him as *Jesus the freedom fighter*, the urban guerrilla, the first-century Che Guevara, with black beard and flashing eyes, whose most characteristic gesture was to overthrow the tables of the moneychangers and to drive them out of the temple with a whip.

These different portraits illustrate the recurring tendency to update Christ in line with current fashions. It began in the apostolic age, with Paul needing to warn of false teachers who were preaching 'a Jesus other than the Jesus we [apostles] preached'.[5] Each succeeding generation tends to read back into him its own ideas and hopes, and create him in its own image.

Their motive is right (to paint a contemporary portrait of Jesus), but the result is always distorted (as the portrait is unauthentic). The challenge before us is to present Jesus to our generation in ways that are both accurate and appealing.

Calling for double listening

The main reason for every betrayal of the authentic Jesus is that we pay too much attention to contemporary trends and too little to God's Word. The thirst for relevance becomes so demanding that we feel we have to give in to it, whatever the cost. We become slaves to the latest fad, prepared to sacrifice truth on the altar of modernity. The quest for relevance degenerates into a lust for popularity. For the opposite extreme to irrelevance is accommodation, a feeble-minded, unprincipled surrender to the spirit of the time.

God's people live in a world which can be actively hostile. We are constantly exposed to the pressure to conform.

Thank God, however, that there have always been those who have stood firm, sometimes alone, and refused to compromise. I think of Jeremiah in the sixth century BC, and Paul in his day ('everyone . . . has deserted me'),[6] Athanasius in the fourth century and Luther in the sixteenth.

In our own day we too need to resolve to present the biblical gospel in such a way as to speak to modern dilemmas, fears and frustrations, but with equal determination not to compromise it in so doing. Some stumbling-blocks are intrinsic to the original gospel and cannot be eliminated or soft-pedalled in order to make it easier to accept. The gospel contains some features so alien to modern thought that it will always appear foolish, however hard we strive to show that it is 'true and reasonable'.[7] The cross will always be an assault on human self-righteousness and a challenge to human self-indulgence. Its 'scandal' (stumbling-block) simply cannot be removed. The church speaks most authentically not when it has become indistinguishable from the world around us, but when its distinctive light shines most brightly.

However keen we are to communicate God's Word to others, we must be faithful to that Word and, if necessary, be prepared to suffer for it. God's word to Ezekiel encourages us: 'Do not be afraid of them . . . You must speak my words to them, whether they listen or fail to listen, for they are rebellious.'[8] Our calling is to be faithful and relevant, not merely trendy.

How then can we develop a Christian mind which is both shaped by the truths of historic, biblical Christianity and also fully immersed in the realities of the contemporary world? We have to begin with a double refusal. We refuse to become either so absorbed in the Word that we *escape* into it and fail to let it confront the world, or so absorbed in the world that we *conform* to it and fail to subject it to the judgment of the Word.

In place of this double refusal, we are called to double listening. We need to listen to the Word of God with expectancy and humility, ready for God perhaps to confront us with a word that may be disturbing and uninvited. And we must also listen to the world around us. The voices we hear may take the form of shrill and strident protest. There will also be the anguished cries of those who are suffering, and the pain, doubt, anger, alienation and even despair of those who are at odds with God. We listen to the Word with humble reverence, anxious to understand it, and resolved to believe and obey what we come to understand. We listen to the world with critical alertness, anxious to understand it too, and resolved not necessarily to believe and obey it, but to sympathize with it and to seek grace to discover how the gospel relates to it.

Everybody finds listening difficult. But are Christians sometimes less good at listening than others? We can learn from the so-called 'comforters' in the Old Testament book of Job. They began well. When they heard about Job's troubles, they came to visit him and, seeing how great his sufferings were, said nothing to him for a whole week. If only they had continued as they began, and kept their mouths shut! Instead, they trotted out their conventional view – that every sinner suffers for his or her own sins – in the most insensitive way. They did not really listen to what Job had to say. They merely repeated their own thoughtless and heartless claptrap, until in the end God stepped in and rebuked them for having misrepresented him.

We need to cultivate 'double listening', the ability to listen to two voices at the same time – the voice of God through the Bible and the voices of men and women around us. These voices will often contradict one another, but our purpose in listening to them both is to discover how they relate to each other. Double listening is indispensable to Christian discipleship and to Christian mission.

It is only through this discipline of double listening that it is possible to become a 'contemporary Christian'. We bring 'historical' and 'contemporary' together as we learn to apply the Word to the world, proclaiming good news which is both true and new.

To put it in a nutshell, we live in the 'now' in the light of the 'then'.

The Church
Introduction

John Wesley was right when he described Christianity as essentially a 'social' religion, and added that to turn it into a 'solitary' religion would be to destroy it. This is not to deny that it offers individual salvation and calls people to individual discipleship. It is rather to affirm that the church lies at the centre of God's purpose. Christ gave himself for us, we are told, not only 'to redeem us from all wickedness', but also 'to purify for himself a people that are his very own, eager to do what is good'.[1]

The problem we have when we think about the church is the tension between the ideal and the reality. The ideal is beautiful. The church is the chosen and beloved people of God, his own special treasure, the covenant community to whom he has committed himself for ever. It is engaged in continuous worship of God and in compassionate outreach to the world, a haven of love and peace, and a pilgrim people headed for the eternal city. But in reality we who claim to be the church are often a motley rabble of rather scruffy individuals, half-educated and half-saved, uninspired in our worship, constantly bickering with each other. We are concerned more for our maintenance than our mission, struggling and stumbling along the road, needing constant rebuke and exhortation, which are readily available from both Old Testament prophets and New Testament apostles.

This distinction between the ideal and the reality means that people's opinions of the church vary enormously. On the one hand, P. T. Forsyth could write that 'the church of Christ is the greatest and finest product of human history ... the greatest thing in the universe'.[2] On the other, Thomas Arnold wrote, 'The church as it now

9

stands no human power can save . . . When I think of the church, I could sit down and pine and die.'[3]

My purpose in this book is to focus on the ideal, on what God intends his church to be, while all the time keeping in view the reality, so that we can grasp the changes which need to be made. The first two chapters are complementary, since we consider in chapter 1 the world's challenge to the church and in chapter 2 the church's mission in the world. In chapter 3 the renewal the church's needs will be seen to include, as Jesus prayed, not only one area (e.g. its unity or its spirituality), but every area of its life. And to this end, those of us who have been ordained to the pastoral ministry of the church need ourselves to be renewed according to God's purpose, which is the topic of chapter 4.

1

Secular challenges to the church

One of the church's greatest needs is a sensitive awareness of the world around us. If we are true servants of Jesus Christ, we will keep our eyes open (as he did) to human need, and our ears alert to cries of anguish. We will respond compassionately and constructively (as again he did) to people's pain.

This does not mean that in every respect we 'let the world set the agenda for the church', as people used to say, or that we trot like a little dog at the world's heels. To behave like that would be to confuse service (which is our calling) with servility (which is not), and to interpret sensitivity (which is a virtue) as conformity (which is a vice). No, first and foremost we have to declare and do what God has sent us to declare and do. We are not to pay fawning homage to the world.

At the same time, unless we listen attentively to the voices of secular society, struggle to understand them, and feel with people in their frustration, anger, bewilderment and despair, we will lack authenticity as the disciples of Jesus of Nazareth. We will run the risk of answering questions nobody is asking, scratching where nobody is itching, supplying goods for which there is no demand – in other words, of being totally irrelevant, as we began to see in our Introduction.

This chapter explores the threefold quest of modern, secular people, which in fact reflects universal human aspirations. They are hopes which Jesus Christ himself arouses in people, which he alone can satisfy, and which challenge the church to present him to the world in his fullness.

The quest for transcendence

Until quite recently, many assumed that secularism would gradually expel any religious sensibilities from society. 'Transcendence' was seen as a rather obscure word whose use was limited to institutions of theological learning. There students were introduced to the distinction between 'transcendence' (meaning God above and outside the created world) and 'immanence' (meaning God present and active within it). But increasingly people are recognizing that even in modern cultures the quest for transcendence goes on. This quest is a kind of protest against secularization, that is, against the attempt to eliminate God from our own world. Human beings do not 'live on bread alone', for materialism cannot satisfy the human spirit. Consider some examples of the recent disillusionment with secularism and the persistent search for transcendence.

First, there was *the collapse of European Marxism* in the late 1980s and early 1990s. Marxism was originally presented as a substitute for outmoded religious faith. But converts were few and far between. As Canon Trevor Beeson wrote about Eastern Europe, 'the basic doctrines of Communism have neither convinced the minds, nor satisfied the emotions, of the intelligentsia or of the proletariat. On the other hand, religious life has displayed remarkable resilience and, far from disappearing, has in many instances found new vitality and power.'[1] The Russian writer Aleksandr Solzhenitsyn drew attention to something which the leaders of the former Soviet Union had not expected:

> that in a land where churches have been levelled, where a triumphant atheism has rampaged uncontrolled for two-thirds of a century, where clergy are utterly humiliated and deprived of all independence, where what remains of the church as an institution is tolerated only for the sake of propaganda directed at the West, where even today people are sent to the labour

camps for their faith, and where, within the camps themselves, those who gather to pray at Easter are clapped in punishment cells – they [i.e. the Soviet leaders] could not suppose that beneath this communist steam-roller the Christian tradition could survive in Russia! But there remain many millions of believers; it is only external pressures that keep them from speaking out.[2]

The second sphere in which people are seen to be disillusioned with secularism is *the desert of Western materialism*. Secularism is no more satisfying to the human spirit in its capitalist, than in its communist, guise. Theodore Roszak is an eloquent American exponent of its emptiness. The significant subtitle of his book *Where the Wasteland Ends* is *Politics and Transcendence in a Post-Industrial Society*.[3] He laments what he calls the 'coca-colonization of the world'.[4] We are suffering, he writes, from 'a psychic claustrophobia within the scientific worldview' in which the human spirit cannot breathe.[5] He castigates science (pseudo-science, I think he means) for its arrogant claim to be able to explain everything, its 'debunking spirit',[6] its 'undoing of the mysteries'. 'For what science can measure is only a portion of what man can know.'[7] This materialistic world of objective science, he goes on, is not nearly 'spacious enough' for us.[8] Without transcendence 'the person shrivels'.[9] His prescription (the recovery of Blake's 'visionary imagination') is woefully inadequate, but his diagnosis is right on target. Human beings know instinctively that Reality cannot be confined in a test tube, or reduced to data in server farms, or apprehended through cool scientific detachment. For life has another and transcendent dimension, and Reality is 'awesomely vast'.[10]

Third, the quest for transcendence is seen in *the epidemic of drug abuse*. There are, of course, a number of different interpretations of this almost worldwide phenomenon. In part, it can be an innocent experimentation, or a protest against conventional mores, or even an attempt to escape the harsh realities of life. But it can also be a genuine search for a 'higher consciousness', and even for an objective transcendent reality. Carlos Castaneda, for example, describes how he used drugs as a form of 'divination', bodily flight or bodilessness, adopting alternative bodies, and moving into and through objects. Clearly not every drug user is pursuing such a distinctive path, but many are trying to escape the boredom of the mundane.[11]

The fourth example of the quest for transcendence is *the proliferation of religious cults*. Alongside the resurgence of ancient faiths has gone the emergence of new religions. The American clinical psychologist, Professor Margaret Singer, estimates that 2 million people are involved in around 5,000 separate cults in the United States alone.[12] A leading article in *The Economist* warned that 'a groping has begun for new forms of spiritual experience'. It added, 'In that search for God, it is all too easy to blunder into the arms of Satan instead.'[13] Peter Berger, the sociologist, has given a similar explanation: 'The current occult wave (including its devil component) is to be understood as resulting from the repression of transcendence in modern consciousness.'[14]

Most striking of all recent religious trends is the rise of the New Age movement. It is a bizarre assortment of diverse beliefs, religion and science, physics and metaphysics, ancient pantheism and evolutionary optimism, astrology, spiritism, reincarnation, ecology and alternative medicine. One of the movement's leaders, David Spangler, writes in his book *Emergence: The Rebirth of the Sacred* that 'from a very early age' he had himself been 'aware of an extra dimension' to the world around him, which as he grew older he came to identify as 'a sacred or transcendental dimension'. 'The rebirth of the sense of the sacred,' he adds, 'is at the heart of the new age.'[15]

Here, then, are four contemporary pieces of evidence that materialism does not satisfy the human spirit, and that as a result people are looking for another, a transcendent, reality. They seek it everywhere – through yoga and the Eastern religions, through sex (which Malcolm Muggeridge used to call 'the mysticism of the materialist'), through music and the other arts, through a drug-induced higher consciousness, through modern cults, New Age speculations, the fantasies of science fiction, and the immersive experience of online gaming and virtual reality.

The immediate Christian reaction to this complex phenomenon should be one of sympathy. For we surely understand what is going on, and why. In the words of the apostle Paul before the Athenian philosophers, men and women are 'feeling after God', like blind people in the dark, groping after their Creator, who leaves them restless until they find their rest in him.[16] They are expressing the human quest for transcendence.

This quest for transcendence is a challenge to the quality of the church's public worship. Does it offer what people are craving – the element of mystery, a sense of holiness, in biblical language 'the fear of God', in modern language 'transcendence'? My answer is, 'Not often.' The church is not always conspicuous for the profound reality of its worship. In particular, we who call ourselves 'evangelical' do not know much how to worship. Evangelism is our speciality, not worship. We seem to have little sense of the greatness and the glory of Almighty God. We do not bow down before him in awe and wonder. Our tendency is to be cocky, flippant and proud. We take little trouble to prepare our worship services. Sometimes they are slovenly, mechanical, perfunctory and dull. At other times they are frivolous to the point of irreverence. No wonder those seeking Reality often pass us by!

We need to listen again to the biblical criticism of religion. No book, not even by Marx and his followers, is more scathing of empty religion than the Bible. The prophets of the eighth and seventh centuries BC were outspoken in their attack on the formalism and hypocrisy of Israelite worship. Jesus applied their critique to the Pharisees of his day: 'These people . . . honour me with their lips, but their hearts are far from me.'[17] And this indictment of religion by the

Old Testament prophets and by Jesus is uncomfortably applicable to us and our churches today. Too much of our worship is ritual without reality, form without power, fun without fear, religion without God.

What is needed then? Here are some suggestions. First, we need such a faithful reading and preaching of God's Word that through it his living voice is heard, addressing his people. Second, we need such a reverent and expectant administration of the Lord's Supper that (I choose my words carefully) there is a Real Presence of Jesus Christ, not in the elements, but among his people and at his table. There should be a sense of Jesus Christ himself, objectively and really present, coming to meet us, ready to make himself known to us through the breaking of bread, and anxious to give himself to us, so that we may feed on him in our hearts by faith. Third, we need such a sincere offering of praise and prayer that God's people say with Jacob, 'Surely the LORD is in this place, and I was not aware of it',[18] and unbelievers will fall down and worship God, exclaiming, 'God is really among you!'[19]

In summary, it is a great tragedy that people today who are seeking transcendence turn to drugs, sex, cults, mysticism, the New Age and science fiction, instead of to the church, in whose worship services true transcendence should always be experienced, and a close encounter with the living God enjoyed.

The quest for significance

There is much in the modern world which not only smothers our sense of transcendence, but also undermines our sense of personal significance, our belief that life has any meaning.

First, there is the effect of *technology*. Technology can be liberating, of course, insofar as it frees people from domestic or industrial drudgery. But it can also be dreadfully dehumanizing, as people feel they are no longer persons but things, their lives processed by inanimate computers and their personalities reduced to data sets.

Second, there is *scientific reductionism*. Some scientists argue that a human being is nothing but an animal (what Dr Desmond Morris calls the 'naked ape'), or nothing but a DNA sequence, programmed to make automatic responses to external stimuli. Statements like these prompted Professor Donald MacKay to popularize the expression 'nothing buttery' (human beings are 'nothing but . . .') as an explanation of what is meant by 'reductionism', and to protest against this tendency to make human beings less than the fully personal.

To be sure, our brain is a highly complex machine, and our anatomy is that of an animal. But that is not a complete account of our humanness. There is more to us than a brain and a body.

Third, *existentialism* diminishes people's sense of significance. Radical existentialists differ from other humanists in their resolve to take their atheism seriously and face its terrible consequences. Because (in their view) God is dead, everything else has died with him. Because there is no God, there are now no values or ideals either, no moral laws or standards, no purposes or meanings – except those which individuals create for themselves as they go along. There is nothing that gives my existence any significance except my decision to seek the courage to be. Meaning is found only in despising my own meaninglessness. There is no other way to authenticate myself.

Bleakly heroic as this philosophy may sound, there must be few people able to perform the conjuring trick of pretending to have significance when they know they have none. For significance is basic to survival. This is what Viktor Frankl found in the Auschwitz concentration camp. He noticed that the inmates most likely to survive were those 'who knew that there was a task waiting for them to fulfil'.[20] Later he became Professor of Psychiatry and Neurology at the University of Vienna and founded the so-called 'Third Viennese School of Psychiatry'. He claimed that, in addition to Freud's 'will to pleasure' and Adler's 'will to power', human beings have a 'will to meaning'. Indeed, 'the striving to find a meaning in one's life is the primary motivational force in man'.[21] 'The mass neurosis of the present time', he wrote, is 'the existential vacuum',[22] that is, the loss of a sense that life is meaningful. He would sometimes ask his clients, 'Why don't you commit suicide?' (an extraordinary question for a doctor to put to a patient!). They would reply that there was something (perhaps their work or marriage or family) which made life worthwhile for them. Professor Frankl would then build on this.

Meaninglessness can lead to boredom, alcoholism, delinquency and suicide. Commenting on Viktor Frankl's work, Arthur Koestler wrote,

> It is an inherent tendency in man to reach out for *meanings* to fulfil and for *values* to actualize ... Thousands and thousands of young students are exposed to an indoctrination ... which denies the existence of values. The result is a worldwide phenomenon – more and more patients are crowding our clinics with the complaint of an inner emptiness, the sense of a total and ultimate meaninglessness of life.[23]

According to Émile Durkheim, in his classic study of suicide, the greatest number of suicides are caused by 'normlessness' or 'meaninglessness', when somebody either has no goal in life or pursues an unattainable goal. 'No human being can be happy or even exist unless his needs are sufficiently proportioned to his means.'[24]

If the quest for transcendence was a challenge to the quality of the church's worship, the quest for significance is a challenge to the quality of the church's teaching. Millions of people do not know who they are, nor that they have any significance or worth. Hence the urgent challenge to tell them who they are, to enlighten them about their identity. We need to teach without compromise the full biblical doctrine of our human being – its depravity, yes, but also its dignity.

Christians believe in the intrinsic worth of human beings, because of our doctrines of creation and redemption. God made humanity in his own image and gave us a responsible stewardship of the earth and its creatures. He has endowed us with rational, moral, social, creative and spiritual faculties which make us like him and unlike the animals. Human beings are Godlike beings. As a result of the fall, our Godlikeness has been distorted, but it has not been destroyed. Furthermore, 'God so loved the world' that he gave his only Son for our redemption. The cross is the chief public evidence of the value which God places on us.

Christian teaching on the dignity and worth of human beings is of the utmost importance today, not only for the sake of our own self-image and self-respect, but even for the welfare of society as a whole.

When human beings are devalued, everything in society turns sour. Women are humiliated, and children despised. The sick are regarded as a nuisance, and the elderly as a burden. Ethnic minorities are discriminated against. The poor are oppressed and denied social justice. Capitalism displays its ugliest face. Labour is exploited in the mines and factories. Criminals are brutalized in prison. Opposition opinions are stifled. Concentration camps like Belsen are invented by the extreme Right, and forced labour camps like the Gulag by the extreme Left. Unbelievers are left to live and die in their lostness. There is no freedom, no dignity, no carefree joy. Human life seems not worth living, because it is scarcely human any longer.

But when human beings are valued as persons, because of their intrinsic worth, everything changes. Men, women and children are all honoured. The sick are cared for, and the elderly enabled to live and die with dignity. Dissidents are listened to, prisoners rehabilitated, minorities protected and the oppressed set free. Workers are given a fair wage, decent working conditions and a measure of participation in both the management and the profit of the enterprise. And the gospel is taken to the ends of the earth. Why? Because people matter. Because every man, woman and child has worth and significance as a human being made in God's image and likeness.

The quest for community

The modern technocratic society, which destroys transcendence and significance, also destroys community. We are living in an era of social disintegration. People find it difficult to relate to one another. Yet we go on seeking the very thing which eludes us – love in a loveless world. I summon as my witnesses three very different people.

The first is Mother Teresa. Born in Skopje, the capital of the Republic of Macedonia, she left for India when she was only seventeen years old. Then, after about twenty years of teaching, she began to serve the poorest of the poor in Calcutta. The same year (1948) she became an Indian citizen, and two years later founded her own order, the 'Missionaries of Charity'. So India was her home for over sixty years. This is what she wrote about the West:

> People today are hungry for love, for understanding love, which is . . . the only answer to loneliness and great poverty. That is why we [i.e. the sisters and brothers of her order] are able to go to countries like England and America and Australia, where there is no hunger for bread. But there people are suffering from terrible loneliness, terrible despair, terrible hatred, feeling unwanted, feeling helpless, feeling hopeless. They have forgotten how to smile, they have forgotten the beauty of the human touch. They are forgetting what is human love. They need someone who will understand and respect them.[25]

I remember that when I first read this assessment of the Western world, I was a bit indignant and considered it exaggerated. But I have since changed my mind. I think it is accurate, at least as a generalization.

My second witness is Bertrand Russell, the brilliant mathematician and philosopher, and uncompromising atheist. He wrote with moving candour in the Prologue to his autobiography:

> Three passions, simple but overwhelmingly strong, have governed my life: the longing for love, the search for knowledge, and unbearable pity for the suffering of mankind. These passions, like great winds, have blown me hither and thither, in a wayward course, over a deep ocean of anguish, reaching to the very verge of despair. I have sought love, first, because it brings ecstasy ... I have sought it, next, because it relieves loneliness – that terrible loneliness in which one's shivering consciousness looks over the rim of the world into the cold unfathomable lifeless abyss ...[26]

Woody Allen is my third witness. Most people think of him as a comedian (he was selling jokes to the press while he was still at high school), but 'inside the clown there's a tragedian'.[27] For all his acclaimed brilliance as an author, director and actor, he never seems to have found either himself or anybody else. He describes love-making as 'two psychopaths under one quilt'. In his film *Manhattan* (1979), he quips that he thinks people ought to 'mate for life, like pigeons or Catholics', but he appears unable to follow his own precept. He confesses that all his films 'deal with that greatest of all difficulties – love relationships. Everybody encounters that. People are either in love, about to fall in love, on the way out of love, looking for love, or a way to avoid it.'[28] His biographer ends his portrait of him with these words: 'He is struggling, as *we* are surely struggling, to find the strength to found a life upon a love. As the character says in *Hannah and Her Sisters*, "Maybe the poets are right. Maybe love is the only answer."'[29]

Here are three people of very different backgrounds, beliefs, temperaments and experiences, who nevertheless agree with one another about the paramount importance of love. They speak for the human race. We all know instinctively that love is indispensable to our humanness. Love is what life is all about.

So people are seeking it everywhere. Some are breaking away from Western individualism and experimenting with communal styles of living. Others are repudiating the age-long institutions of marriage and the family in an attempt (vain and foolish, Christians believe) to find the freedom and spontaneity of love. Everybody is searching for genuine community and the authentic relationships of love. The well-known words of 'Love, love changes everything' from Andrew Lloyd Webber's musical *Aspects of Love* say it all.

The world's third challenge, then, concerns the quality of the church's fellowship. We proclaim that God is love, and that Jesus Christ offers true community. We insist that the church is part of the gospel. God's purpose, we say, is not merely to save isolated individuals, and so perpetuate their loneliness, but to build a church, to create a new society, even a new humanity, in which racial, national, social and sexual barriers have been abolished. Moreover, this new community of Jesus dares to present itself as the true alternative society, which eclipses the values and standards of the world.

It is a high-sounding claim. But the tragedy is that the church has consistently failed to live up to its own ideals. Its theological understanding of its calling may be impeccable. But, comparatively speaking, there is little acceptance, little caring and little supportive love among us. People searching for community ought to be pouring into our churches. Instead, the church is the one place they do not bother to check out, so sure are they that they will not find love there.

It would be unjust, however, to be entirely negative in our evaluation of the contemporary church. For there are Christian communities all over the world where true, sacrificial, serving, supportive love is to be found. Where such Christian love flourishes, its magnetism is almost irresistible. Bishop Stephen Neill expressed it well:

> Within the fellowship of those who are bound together by personal loyalty to Jesus Christ, the relationship of love reaches an intimacy and intensity unknown elsewhere. Friendship between the friends of Jesus of Nazareth is unlike any other friendship. This ought to be normal experience within the Christian community . . . That in existing Christian congregations it is so rare is a measure of the failure of the church as a whole to live up to the purpose of its Founder for it. Where it is experienced, especially across the barriers of race, nationality and language, it is one of the most convincing evidences of the continuing activity of Jesus among men.[30]

Here, then, is a threefold quest on which human beings are engaged. Although people might not articulate like this, we may say that in looking for transcendence they are trying to find God, in looking for significance they are trying to find themselves, and in looking for community they are trying to find their neighbour. This is humankind's universal search for God, our neighbour and ourselves.

Moreover, it is the Christian claim (confident I know, humble I hope) that those who seek will find – in Christ and in his new society. The contemporary secular quest seems to me to constitute one of the greatest challenges – and opportunities – with which the church has ever been presented: people are openly looking for the very things that Jesus Christ is offering!

The only question is whether the church can be so radically renewed by the Spirit and the Word of God that it offers an experience of transcendence through its worship, of significance through its teaching, and of community through its fellowship. If it can, then people will turn to it eagerly, and our proclamation of the good news will have a credibility which otherwise it lacks.

Reflection questions from Tim Chester

1 What are the hopes, fears and frustrations of the people around you?
2 How are these hopes and fears met in Christ and his people?
3 What signs of a desire for transcendence do you see in our culture?
4 How can we ensure that a sense of transcendence is a feature of the worship of our churches?
5 Where do the people around you look for meaning? How does the gospel confirm, complete or challenge these attempts to find meaning?
6 Which practical steps could you take to ensure your church or small group is a community of magnetic love?

2

Evangelism through the local church[1]

'If any man be a dumb Christian, not professing his faith openly, but cloaking and colouring himself for fear of danger in time to come, he giveth men occasion, justly and with good conscience, to doubt lest he have not the grace of the Holy Ghost within him, because he is tongue tied and doth not speak.' In other words, Christians who never share their faith are unlikely to be true Christians. So said the *Second Book of Homilies*, a 1571 collection of sermons to be read out in churches to introduce the people of England to the newly Reformed faith of the church.

Various forms of evangelism

Evangelism can take different forms. Ever since Jesus offered living water to the Samaritan woman at Jacob's well,[2] and Philip told the good news of Jesus to the Ethiopian in his chariot,[3] *personal evangelism* has had impeccable biblical precedents. It is still our duty, when the opportunity is given, to share Christ with our relatives, friends, neighbours and colleagues who do not yet know him.

Mass evangelism too (the preaching of an evangelist to crowds) has over the centuries been blessed by God. Jesus himself proclaimed the good news of the kingdom to the crowds in Galilee. So did the apostle Paul to the pagans of Lystra[4] and the philosophers of Athens.[5] So did John Wesley and George Whitefield in eighteenth-century Britain and America. Gifted evangelists of many nationalities are still preaching effectively to large crowds today, although they know that their ministry depends on the cooperation of churches and Christians. And all over the world there are clergy and lay people who take preaching seriously, and who remember that their congregation will often include both non-Christians and nominal Christians who need to hear the gospel.

Nevertheless, *local church evangelism* is the most normal, natural and productive method of spreading the gospel today, for two main reasons.

First, there is *the argument from Scripture*. According to the apostle Peter, the church is both 'a royal priesthood' to offer spiritual sacrifices to God (which is worship) and 'a holy nation' to proclaim God's praises (which is witness).[6] And these responsibilities of the universal church devolve to each local church. Every Christian congregation is called by God to be a worshipping, witnessing community. Indeed, each of these two duties necessarily involves the other. If we truly worship God, we find ourselves impelled to make him known to others, so that they may worship him too. Thus worship leads to witness, and witness in turn leads to worship, in a perpetual circle.

The Thessalonians set a fine example of local church evangelism. In his first letter to them Paul points out this remarkable sequence: 'Our gospel came to you . . . You welcomed the message . . . The Lord's message rang out from you.'[7] In this way the local church becomes like a sounding board which reflects and amplifies the vibrations it receives. Or it is like a communications satellite which first accepts and then transmits a message. Every church which has heard the gospel must pass it on. This is still God's principal method of evangelism. If all churches had been faithful to this commission, then the world would long ago have been evangelized.

Second, there is *the argument from strategy*. Each local church is situated in a particular neighbourhood. Its first missional responsibility must therefore be to the people who live there. The congregation is strategically placed to reach the locality. Any political party would be wildly jealous of the plant and personnel which are at our disposal. In many countries the churches have ample resources to disseminate the gospel throughout their land.

Thus biblical theology and practical strategy combine to make the local church the primary agent of evangelism.

But if the local church is to act out its God-appointed role, it must first fulfil four conditions. It must *understand* itself (the theology of the church), *organize* itself (the structures of the church), *express* itself (the message of the church) and *be* itself (the life of the church).

The church must understand itself

The theology of the church

Many churches are sick because they have a false self-image. They have grasped neither who they are (their identity) nor what they are called to be (their vocation). We all know the importance of an accurate self-image for good mental health. What is true of persons is equally true of churches.

At least two false images of the church are prevalent today. The first false image is *the religious club* (or *introverted Christianity*). According to this view, the local church resembles the local golf club, except that the common interest of its members happens to be God rather than golf. They see themselves as religious people who enjoy doing religious things together. They pay their subscription and reckon they are entitled to certain privileges. In fact, they concentrate on the status and advantages of being club members. They have forgotten – or never known – that, as Archbishop William Temple put it, 'The church is the only co-operative society in the world which exists for the benefit of its non-members.' Instead, they are completely introverted, like an ingrown toenail. To be sure, Temple was guilty of a slight exaggeration, for church members do have a responsibility to each other, as the many 'one another' verses of the New Testament indicate ('love one another', 'encourage one another', 'bear one another's burdens', etc.). Nevertheless, our primary responsibilities are our worship of God and our mission in the world.

At the opposite extreme to the religious club is *the secular mission* (or *religionless Christianity*). In the twentieth century, some Christian thinkers became exasperated by the self-centredness of the church. It seemed to them so absorbed in its own petty domestic affairs that they resolved to abandon it. For the arena of divine service they exchanged the church for the secular city. They were no longer interested in 'worship services', they said, but only in 'worship service'. So they tried to develop a 'religionless Christianity' in which they reinterpreted worship as mission, love for God as love for neighbour, and prayer to God as encounter with people. A similar movement of 'post-evangelicals' or the 'emerging church' abandoned traditional congregations in favour of unstructured Christian communities with a focus on neighbourhood transformation.

How should we evaluate such movements? Their distaste for selfish religion is surely right. Since it is nauseating to God, it ought to sicken us as well. But the concept of 'religionless Christianity' is an unbalanced overreaction. The message of the gospel cannot be adjusted to suit modern sensibilities. And we have no liberty to confuse worship and mission, even though (as we have seen) each involves the other. There is always an element of mission in worship and of worship in mission, but they are not synonymous.

There is a third way to understand the church, which combines what is true in both false images, and which recognizes that we have a responsibility both to worship God and to serve the world. This is *the double identity of the church* (or *incarnational Christianity*). By its 'double identity' I mean that the church is a people who have been both called out of the world to worship God and sent back into the world to witness and serve. These are, in fact, two of the classical 'marks' of the church. According to the first, the church is 'holy', called out to belong to God and to worship him. According to the second, the church is 'apostolic', sent out into the world on its mission. The church is to be simultaneously 'holy' (distinct from the world) and 'worldly' (not in the sense of assimilating the world's values, but in the sense of renouncing other-worldliness and instead becoming immersed in the life of the world). Dr Alec Vidler captured this double identity by referring to its 'holy worldliness'.[8]

Nobody has ever exhibited 'holy worldliness' better than our Lord Jesus Christ himself. His incarnation is the perfect embodiment of it. On the one hand, he came to us in our world, and assumed the full reality of our humanness. He made himself one with us in our frailty, and exposed himself to our temptations. He fraternized with the common people, and they flocked round him eagerly. He welcomed everybody and shunned nobody. He identified with our sorrows, our sins and our death. On the other hand, in mixing freely with people like us, he never sacrificed or compromised his own unique identity. His was the perfection of 'holy worldliness'.

And now he sends us into the world as he was sent into the world.[9] We have to penetrate other people's worlds, as he penetrated ours – the world of their thinking (as we struggle to understand their misunderstandings of the gospel), the world of their feeling (as we try to empathize with their pain), and the world of their living (as we sense the humiliation of their social situation, whether that is poverty, homelessness, unemployment or discrimination). Archbishop Michael Ramsey put it well: 'We state and commend the faith only insofar as we go out and put ourselves with loving sympathy inside the doubts of the doubter, the questions of the questioner, and the loneliness of those who have lost the way.'[10] Yet this costly entry into other people's worlds is not to be undertaken at the expense of our own Christian integrity. We are called to maintain the standards of Jesus Christ untarnished.

Seldom in its long history has the church managed to preserve its God-given double identity of holy worldliness. Instead, it has tended to oscillate between the two extremes. Sometimes (in an overemphasis on its holiness) the church has withdrawn from the world and so has neglected its mission. At other times (in an overemphasis on its worldliness) it has conformed to the world, assimilating its views and values, and so has neglected its holiness. But to fulfil its mission, the church must faithfully respond to both its callings, and preserve both parts of its identity.

'Mission' arises, then, from the biblical doctrine of the church in the world. If we are not 'the church', the holy and distinct people of God, we have nothing to say because we are compromised. If, on the other hand, we are not 'in the world', deeply involved in its life and suffering, we have no-one to serve because we are insulated. Our calling is to be 'holy' and 'worldly' at the same time. Without this balanced biblical ecclesiology, we will never recover or fulfil our mission.

The church must organize itself

The structures of the church

The church must organize itself in a way that expresses its under-standing of itself. Its structures must reflect its theology, especially its double identity.

Often the church is structured for 'holiness' rather than 'worldliness', for worship and fellowship rather than mission. In contrast, the report *The Church for Others: A Quest for Structures for Missionary Congregations* says,

> The missionary church is not concerned with itself – it is a church for others ... Its centre lies outside itself; it must live 'excentredly' ... The church has to turn itself outwards to the world... We have to recognize that the churches have developed into 'waiting churches' into which people are expected to come.

Its inherited structures stress and embody this static outlook. One may say that we are in danger of perpetuating 'come-structures' instead of replacing them by 'go-structures'. One may say that inertia has replaced the dynamism of the gospel and of participation in the mission of God.[11]

Our static, inflexible, self-centred structures are 'heretical structures' because they embody a heretical doctrine of the church.

Some zealous churches organize an overfull programme of church-based activities with something arranged for every night of the week. On Monday night the committees meet, and on Tuesday night it's the fellowship groups. On Wednesday night there's a Bible study, while Thursday night is the prayer meeting. On Friday and Saturday evenings other good causes occupy people's time and energy. Such churches give the impression that their main goal is to keep their members out of mischief!

But such a crowded, church-centred programme, admirable as it may look at first sight, has many drawbacks and dangers. To begin with, it is detrimental to family life. Marriages break up and families disintegrate because parents are seldom at home. It also inhibits church members from getting involved in the local community because they are so preoccupied with the local church. In this way it contradicts an essential part of the church's identity, its 'worldliness'. As Bishop Richard Wilke has put it, 'Our structure has become an end in itself, not a means of saving the world.'[12] In that case, it is a heretical structure.

I sometimes wonder (although I exaggerate to make my point) if it would not be more healthy for church members to meet only on Sundays (for worship, fellowship and teaching) and not at all midweek. Then we would gather on Sundays and scatter for the rest of the week. We would come to Christ for worship and go for Christ in mission. And in that rhythm of Sunday–weekday, gathering–scattering, coming–going and worship–mission, the church would express its holy worldliness, and its structure would conform to its double identity.

How, then, should the local church organize itself? Ideally, it seems to me, every five or ten years each church should evaluate itself and review how far its structures reflect its identity. It should conduct a 'local church audit' to review how far the church is penetrating the community for Christ. This could involve two surveys, to create a 'parish profile' ('to build up an accurate picture of the parish') and a 'church profile' ('to build up an accurate picture of the local church').[13]

A local community survey

Each church is set in a particular situation, and needs to become familiar with its context. This involves asking questions like these:

1 What sort of people live in our parish or locality? What is their ethnic origin, nationality, religion, culture, media preference and work? What proportion are two-parent families, single-parent families, single people, senior citizens, young people? What are the area's main housing, employment, economic and educational needs?

2 Has the locality any centres of education, including schools, colleges, adult education centres or playgroups?

3 What businesses are found in the area? Factories, farms, offices, shops or studios? Is there significant unemployment?

4 Where do people live? Do they occupy houses or flats? Do they own or rent their homes? Are there any hotels, hostels, student residences, apartment blocks or care homes?

5 Where do people congregate when they are at leisure? Café or restaurant, pub or nightclub, shopping mall, youth club or other clubs, bingo hall, concert hall, theatre or cinema, sports ground, park or street corner?

6 What local public services exist? Police, fire brigade, prison, hospital, public library, other social services?

7 Are there other religious buildings – church or chapel, syna-
gogue, mosque, temple or Christian Science reading room?
8 Has the community changed in the last ten years, and what
changes can be forecast for the next ten?

A local church survey

This second survey needs to ask whether the church is organized to
serve itself, or to serve God and the community. Is it really organized
only for itself, for its own survival and convenience, and for the
preservation of its privileges? What are its cherished traditions and
conventions which unnecessarily separate it from the community?

1 *The church building.* Church members tend to be most interested
in its *interior* (its beauty, comfort and amenities). But we also
need to walk round it and look at it through the eyes of an
outsider: what image does it present? Is it a fortress (dark, for-
bidding and austere), or is it bright, inviting and welcoming? A
critical look at the inside of the church building will be necessary
too, especially through the eyes of non-Christian visitors – its
decoration and furniture, lighting and heating, its noticeboards,
posters, bookstall and leaflets.

2 *The church services.* Are our services exclusively for the committed, designed only for the initiated, and therefore mumbo-
jumbo to outsiders? Or do we remember the fringe members and
non-members who may be present? What about the forms of
service, the liturgy and language, the music (words, tunes and
instruments), the seating, and the dress of both clergy and congregation? We need to ask ourselves what messages all these
things give out.

3 *The church membership.* Is our membership mobilized for
mission? Or is our church too clergy-dominated so as to make
this impossible? Has it grasped the New Testament's commitment
to 'every-member ministry of the body of Christ'? Or is it less a

body than a pyramid, with the clergy at the pinnacle and the lay people in their serried ranks of inferiority at the base? Are the members of the church also members of the community? Or are they so preoccupied with church activities or commuter Christianity (travelling long distances to church) that local involvement is difficult or artificial?

4 *The church programme.* Do we imprison our members in the church? Or do we deliberately release them (including leaders) from church commitments to be active for Christ in the community? Do we support them with our interest and prayers? Is the biblical truth of the double identity of the church taught and embodied? Is training available for those who want to commit themselves to Christian service and witness?

The two surveys (of community and church) will need to be studied by the church leadership (clergy and lay). Out of this reflection will grow a renewed strategy for mission. The church can then set both long-term and short-term goals, with a list of priorities. The church may decide that it is suffering from a false self-image and needs biblical teaching on its holy worldliness and the implications of this for mission; or that a training programme is needed to equip members for evangelism; or that church-based activities should be reduced to increase involvement in the community. It might decide to restructure the church building, decor, seating or services; or to organize a visitation of the area in cooperation with other local churches; or to form specialist groups to penetrate particular segments of the locality. For example, a group could adopt a local pub, not to make occasional evangelistic raids into it, but between them (in pairs) to visit it regularly over a long period, to make friends with the people who congregate there. Again, the church may decide to arrange home meetings for neighbours, or a series of apologetics lectures in a neutral building, or regular guest services with an evangelistic thrust, to which members can bring their friends. Or the church may decide to take up some special social need, which has surfaced during the surveys, and encourage a group to study it and then recommend action. All such decisions will be designed to help the church to identify with the community, and to develop structures that facilitate an authentically incarnational mission.

The church must express itself

The message of the church

It is not enough for the local church to understand itself and organize itself accordingly; it must also articulate its message. For evangelism, at its simplest and most basic, is sharing the gospel (the 'evangel'). So in order to define evangelism, we must also define the good news.

There can be no doubt that the essence of the gospel is Jesus Christ himself. It would be impossible to preach the Christian good news without talking about Jesus. So we read that Philip, speaking to the Ethiopian, 'told him the good news about Jesus'.[14] The apostle Paul described himself as 'set apart for the gospel of God ... regarding his Son'.[15] Moreover, in bearing witness to Jesus, we must speak above all of his death and resurrection. To quote Paul's famous summary of the apostolic gospel, 'What I received I passed on to you as of first importance: that Christ died for our sins according to the Scriptures, that he was buried, that he was raised on the third day according to the Scriptures, and that he appeared.'[16] We simply do not share the gospel if we do not declare God's love in the gift of his Son to live our life, to die for our sins and to rise again, together with his offer through Jesus Christ, to all who repent and believe, of a new life of forgiveness and freedom, and of membership in his new society.

But how shall we formulate this good news in our world's increasingly pluralistic societies in such a way that it resonates with them and makes sense? There are two opposite extremes to avoid.

The first extreme I will call *total fixity*. Some Christians seem to be in bondage to words and formula, and so become prisoners of a gospel stereotype. They wrap up their message in a nice, neat package. They tape, label and price-tag it as if it were destined for the supermarket. Then, unless their favourite phraseology is used (whether the kingdom of God, or the blood of Jesus, or human liberation, or being born again, or justification by faith, or the cosmic lordship of Christ), they declare that the gospel has not been preached. What these people seem not to have noticed is the rich diversity of gospel formulations which are found in the New Testament itself. The options I have listed are all biblical, but because all of them contain an element of imagery, and each image is different, it is impossible to fuse them into a single, simple concept. So it is perfectly legitimate to develop one or other of them, according to what seems most appropriate to the occasion.

The opposite extreme is *total fluidity*. Some years ago I heard a British bishop say, 'There's no such thing as the gospel in a vacuum. You don't even know what the gospel is until you enter each particular situation. You have to enter the situation first, and then you discover the gospel when you're there.' Now if he meant that he wanted a gospel in context, not in a vacuum, and that we need to relate the gospel sensitively to each person and situation, I fully agree. But to say that 'there is no such thing as the gospel in a vacuum' and that 'you discover it' in each situation is surely a serious overstatement. For what the advocates of total fluidity seem not to have noticed is that, alongside the New Testament's rich diversity of gospel formulation, there is also an underlying unity (especially regarding the saving death and resurrection of Jesus) which binds the different formulations together. As Professor A. M. Hunter wrote, 'There is . . . a deep unity in the New Testament, which dominates and transcends all the diversities.'[17]

Is there a middle way? Yes, there is. Both the extremes which I have described express important concerns which need to be preserved. The first ('total fixity') rightly emphasizes that the gospel has been revealed by God and received by us. It is both a tradition to be preserved and a deposit to be guarded. We did not invent it, and we have no liberty to edit it or tamper with it. The second ('total fluidity') rightly emphasizes that the gospel must be adapted appropriately to each particular person or situation. Otherwise it will be perceived as irrelevant.

Somehow, then, we have to learn to combine these two proper concerns. We have to wrestle with the tension between the ancient Word and the modern world, between what has been given and what has been left open, between content and context, Scripture and culture, revelation and contextualization. We need more fidelity to Scripture and more sensitivity to people. Not one without the other, but both.

The church must be itself

The life of the church

The church is supposed to be God's new society, the living embodiment of the gospel, a sign of the kingdom of God, a demonstration of what human community looks like when it comes under his gracious rule.

In other words, God's purpose is that the good news of Jesus Christ is communicated visually as well as verbally, 'by word and deed'. Every educator knows how much easier it is for human beings to learn through what they see and experience than through what they hear. Or rather, word and deed, hearing and seeing, belong essentially together. This is certainly so in evangelism. People have to see with their own eyes that the gospel we preach has transformed us. As John Poulton put it, 'Christians . . . need to look like what they are talking about. It is *people* who communicate primarily, not words or ideas . . . What communicates now is basically personal authenticity.'[18] If our life contradicts our message, our evangelism will lack all credibility. Indeed, the greatest hindrance to evangelism is lack of integrity in the evangelist.

In 1 John 4:12 it says, 'No one has ever seen God; but if we love one another, God lives in us and his love is made complete in us.' God is invisible. Nobody has ever seen him. All that human beings have ever seen of him is glimpses of his glory.

The invisibility of God is a great problem for faith. It was so for the Jews in the Old Testament. Their heathen neighbours laughed at them for worshipping an invisible God. 'You say you believe in God?' they taunted them. 'Where is he? Come to our temples, and we will show you our gods. They have ears and eyes, hands and feet, and mouths and noses too. But where is your God? We can't see him. Ha, ha, ha!' The Jews found this ridicule hard to bear. Hence the complaint of psalmist and prophet: 'Why do the nations say, "Where is their God?"'[19] Of course Israel had its own apologetic. The idols of the heathen were nothing, only the work of human hands. True, they had mouths, but they could not speak, ears, but could not hear, noses, but could not smell, hands, but could not feel, and feet, but could not walk.[20] Yahweh, on the other hand, although (being spirit) had no mouth, had spoken; although he had no ears, he listened to Israel's prayers; and although he had no hands, he had both created the universe and redeemed his people by his mighty power. At the same time, the people of God longed for him to make himself known to the nations, so that they might see him and believe in him.

The same problem of an unseen God challenges us today, especially those brought up on the scientific method. They are taught to examine everything with their five senses. They are told to suspect anything which cannot be subjected to empirical investigation. So how could it ever be reasonable to believe in an invisible God? 'Let us only see him,' they say, 'and we will believe.'

How, then, has God solved the problem of his own invisibility? First and foremost he has done so by sending his Son into the world. 'No one has ever seen God; the only Son, who is in the bosom of the Father, he has made him known.'[21] As a result, Jesus could say, 'Anyone who has seen me has seen the Father',[22] and Paul could describe him as 'the [visible] image of the invisible God'.[23]

To this people tend to reply, 'That is wonderful, but it happened nearly 2,000 years ago. Is there no way in which the invisible God makes himself visible *today*?' Yes, there is. 'No one has ever seen God.'[24] We read in 1 John 4:12 the same words as in John 1:18. But now John concludes the sentence differently. In the Gospel he wrote that 'the only Son . . . has made him known'. In the Epistle he writes that 'if we love one another, God lives in us and his love is made complete in us'. Because of John's deliberate repetition of the same statement, this can only mean one thing. The invisible God, who once made himself visible in Christ, now makes himself visible in Christians, *if we love one another.*

God is love in his essential being, and has revealed his love in the gift of his Son to live and die for us. Now he calls us to be a community of love. We are called to love each other in the intimacy of his family – especially across the barriers of age and sex, race and rank. And we are called to the world God loves in its alienation, hunger, poverty and pain. It is through the quality of our love that God makes himself visible today.

We cannot proclaim the gospel of God's love with any degree of integrity if we do not exhibit it in our love for others. Perhaps nothing is so damaging to the cause of Christ as a church which is either torn apart by jealousy, rivalry, slander and malice, or preoccupied with its own selfish concerns. Such churches urgently need to be radically renewed in love. It is only if we love one another that the world will believe that Jesus is the Christ and that we are his disciples.[25]

Here, then, are the four main prerequisites for evangelism through the local church:

1 The church must understand itself (theologically), grasping its double identity of holy worldliness.
2 The church must organize itself (structurally), developing a mission strategy that reflects its double identity.
3 The church must express itself (verbally), articulating its gospel in a way that is both faithful to Scripture and relevant to the contemporary world.
4 The church must be itself (morally and spiritually), becoming a community of love through which the invisible God again makes himself visible to the world.

Reflection questions from Tim Chester

1 The church is called to 'holy worldliness'. Can you think of situations where churches or Christians are holy, but insular? What about situations in which they are engaged, but compromised? Where would you place your church on this spectrum? Where would you place yourself?
2 Review the structures and activities of your church. What do they suggest are the priorities of your church? Is there a mismatch with your stated priorities?
3 Review the needs of your local neighbourhood. Are there needs which your church could meet?
4 Are the members of your church mobilized for mission? What could your church do to equip people for mission? Are there things it should stop doing to free people for involvement in the neighbourhood?

5 Think of the way you speak of Christ to unbelievers. Are you inclined to be too formulaic ('total fixity')? Or are you reluctant to speak clearly and faithfully of Christ's death and resurrection ('total fluidity')?

6 In what ways do people see the invisible God in your life? In the life of your church?

3
Dimensions of church renewal

Over the last hundred years or so the church has seen a series of renewal movements, each focusing on a particular aspect of ecclesiastical life. I can think of at least six.

First, at the beginning of the twentieth century the missionary movement received fresh impetus at the World Missionary Conference in Edinburgh in 1910. The church growth movement founded by Dr Donald McGavran, and the Lausanne Movement with its congresses on world evangelization (Lausanne 1974, Manila 1989 and South Africa 2010), have given this considerable further stimulus.

Second, there was the biblical theology movement whose foundation was laid by the emphasis of Karl Barth and Emil Brunner on the 'otherness' of God and his Word. It flourished between 1945 and 1960 under biblical scholars like Gerhard von Rad (Old Testament) and Oscar Cullmann (New Testament), who stressed the inner unity of Scripture.

Next, the ecumenical movement took shape in the formation of the World Council of Churches in Amsterdam in 1948, and stressed the need to unite the churches in their witness to the world.

Fourth, the post-war liturgical movement, especially (though not exclusively) in the Roman Catholic Church, aimed to modernize the worship of the congregation. The Second Vatican Council gave this a further boost.

Fifth, the charismatic movement sought to incorporate the distinctive emphases of Pentecostal churches into mainline denominations, and was concerned for the restoration of spiritual power and spiritual gifts to the body of Christ.

Sixth, the social justice movement, ranging from the cluster of liberation theologies to the recovery of the evangelical social conscience, sought to balance the church's eternal and other-worldly preoccupations with its temporal, this-worldly responsibilities.

Thus mission, theology, unity, worship, power and justice are six legitimate Christian concerns, each of which has gathered round it devoted protagonists. Yet the result has been an unhealthily fragmented agenda. What we need is a holistic or integrated vision of renewal in every dimension of the church's life.

The Roman Catholic word for this, at least since the Second Vatican Council (1963–1965), has been *aggiornamento*, the process of bringing the church up to date to meet the challenges of the modern world. The world is changing rapidly, and if the church is to survive, it must keep pace with this change, albeit without compromising its own standards or conforming to the world's.

Protestants use a different vocabulary to describe the continuous need to restore and refresh the church. Our two favourite words are 'reform', indicating the kind of reformation of faith and life according to Scripture which took place in the sixteenth century, and 'revival', denoting a supernatural visitation of a church or community by God, bringing conviction, repentance, confession, the conversion of sinners and the recovery of backsliders. 'Reformation' usually stresses the power of the Word of God, and 'revival' the power of the Spirit of God. Perhaps we should use the word 'renewal' to describe a movement which combines revival by God's Spirit with reformation by his Word. Since the Word is the Spirit's sword, there is bound to be something lopsided about contemplating one without the other.

For an integrated vision of continuous renewal, we cannot do better than reflect on Jesus' prayer for his people in John 17. Without doubt, this is one of the most profound chapters of the Bible. There are depths here which we will never fathom; all we can do is paddle in the shallows. Here are heights we cannot scale; we can only climb the foothills.

43

Nevertheless, we must persevere. For if the upper-room discourse (John 13 – 17) is the temple of Scripture, John 17 is its inner sanctuary or holy of holies. Here we are introduced to the presence, mind and heart of God. We are permitted to eavesdrop as the Son communes with the Father. We need to take off our shoes, since this is holy ground.

Jesus prays

- for himself as he approaches the cross (verses 1–5);
- for his apostles, to whom he has revealed the Father and who are gathered round him as he prays (verses 6–19);
- for the whole church present and future, consisting of all those who will believe in him through the apostles' teaching (verses 20–26).

We will concentrate on the second and third sections (verses 6–26).

As a matter of fact, Jesus does not begin his prayer for his people until the end of verse 11. Before this, in verses 6–11a he describes the people he is going to pray for. It is quite an elaborate description and, although it refers primarily to the apostles, it concerns them as ordinary disciples rather than in their distinctive apostolic ministry. The description has three parts.

First, *they belong to Christ.* Three times Jesus repeats the truth that the Father has 'given' them to him out of the world (verses 6 and 9), so that they belong to him.

Second, *they know the Father.* For if the Father has given them to the Son, the Son has given them a revelation of the Father. This too is repeated: 'I have revealed you [literally 'your name'] to those whom you gave me out of the world' (verse 6). Also, 'I gave them the words you gave me and they accepted them' (verse 8). Of course this revelation of God's name, this gift of God's words, was made in the first instance to the apostles, but from them it has been passed on to all Christ's disciples.

Third, *they live in the world.* 'I will remain in the world no longer,' Jesus says, 'but they are still in the world, and I am coming to you' (verse 11a). Although they have been given to Christ 'out of the world' (verse 6), they nevertheless remain 'in the world' (verse 11a) out of which they have been taken. They are to be spiritually distinct, but not socially segregated. Jesus leaves them behind as his representatives or ambassadors.

Here, then, is Jesus' threefold characterization of his people, beginning with his apostles, but including all later disciples, reaching even to us. First, the Father has given us to the Son. Second, the Son has revealed to us the Father. Third, we live in the world. It is this threefold orientation (to the Father, to the Son and to the world) which makes us the 'holy' people we are. We live in the world as a people who know God and belong to Christ, and therefore (it is implied) have a unique mission to make him known.

What then does Christ pray for his people whom he has so carefully described? The burden of his intercession consists of only two words, which are repeated. 'Holy Father, *protect them* . . . My prayer is . . . that you *protect them* from the evil one' (verses 11b and 15). It is a prayer that the holy Father will keep us the holy people we are, that he will protect and preserve us from any and every evil influence which might spoil the unique position he has given us. It is a prayer that we may be kept true to who we are, to our essential Christian identity, as a people who know God, belong to Christ and live in the world.

More particularly, Jesus prays that his people may have four characteristics, namely truth, holiness, mission and unity.

Truth (verses 11–13)

A literal translation of verse 11b could be 'Keep them in your name', but commentators are not agreed how to translate the preposition 'in'. The NIV renders it 'Protect them by the power of your name.' Yet the context seems to require that God's name is not so much the power *by* which, as the sphere *in* which, the disciples are to be kept. I think, then, that the Jerusalem Bible is correct to translate it: 'Keep those you have given me true to your name.' The revelation of God's name was 'the enclosing wall, as it were, within which they were to be kept'.[1] For God's name is God himself – who he is, his being and his character. This the Father has revealed to the Son, and the Son in his turn has revealed to the apostles (verse 6). During his earthly ministry, Jesus has kept them in it (verse 12). Now, however, he is about to leave the world. So he prays that the Father will keep them loyal to the name he has revealed to them, 'so that they may be one as we are one' (verse 11). The main means by which they will be united will be their loyalty to God's truth revealed in and through Christ.

Truth, then, was the first concern for his church which Jesus expressed in his prayer. He spoke of revelation, of the disclosure by him of God's otherwise hidden name. He made plain his longing that his people would be loyal to this revelation, and that their unity would be based on their common faithfulness to it. Instead, today I fear that some contemporary church leaders are guilty of serious unfaithfulness. A few are brash enough to deny the fundamentals both of the historic Christian faith and of traditional Christian morality, while others seem as unsure of themselves and their beliefs as a blushing adolescent teenager.

There is no possibility of the church being thoroughly renewed until and unless it is renewed in its commitment to God's revealed truth in Jesus Christ, and in the full biblical testimony to him. Nor is there any chance of the church recovering its unity until it recovers the only authentic basis for unity, which is truth. Jesus prayed first for the truth of the church; we should do the same. For God intends his church to be 'the pillar and foundation of the truth'.[2]

Holiness (verses 14–16)

Jesus prayed that the Father would keep his people not only true to his name, but also 'from the evil one' (verse 15). That is, he desired that they would be preserved on the one hand from error and in truth, and on the other hand from evil and in holiness. The church's final destiny, Paul was later to declare, is to be presented to Christ 'as a radiant church, without stain or wrinkle or any other blemish, but holy and blameless'.[3] But the church's holiness must begin now.

So what is meant by 'holiness'? All down through history the church has tended to go to extremes, as we considered in the last chapter. Sometimes, in its right determination to be holy, it has withdrawn from the world and lost contact with it. At other times, in its equally right determination not to lose contact, it has conformed to the world and become virtually indistinguishable from it. But Christ's vision for the church's holiness is neither withdrawal nor conformity.

Withdrawal was the way of the Pharisees. Anxious to apply the law to the details of everyday life, they had a false understanding of holiness, imagining that mere contact with evil and evil people would bring contamination. And a form of Christian pharisaism or separatism has lingered in the church. It has often been due to a passionate longing for holiness and a zeal to preserve Christian culture from destruction by the wicked world. These motives persuaded the hermits to flee into the desert in the fourth century, and led to the development of medieval monasticism. But, noble as the motives of monks and hermits often were, the kind of monasticism which entailed withdrawal from the world was a betrayal of Christ. So too is the kind of modern piety which imprisons Christians in a ghetto-like fellowship, cutting them off from non-Christians. For Jesus specifically prayed that, although he wanted his disciples to be protected from the evil one, he did not want them to be taken out of the world (verse 15).

If 'withdrawal' was the way of the Pharisees, 'conformity' was the way of the Sadducees. Belonging to wealthy, aristocratic families, they collaborated with the Romans and sought to maintain the political status quo. This compromising tradition also persisted in the early church, and still survives today.

The motive for it can again be good, namely the resolution to break down barriers between the church and the world, and to be the friends of tax collectors and sinners, as Jesus was.[4] But he was also 'set apart from sinners'[5] in his values and standards.

In place of these two extreme positions, Jesus calls us to live 'in the world' (verse 11) while remaining 'not of the world' (verse 14), that is, neither belonging to it, nor imitating its ways. This is the 'holy worldliness' of the church which we explored in the previous chapter. We are neither to give in nor to opt out. Instead, we are to stay in and stand firm, like a rock in a mountain stream, like a rose blooming in mid-winter, like a lily growing in a manure heap.

Mission (verses 17–19)

There are fifteen references to 'the world' in Jesus' prayer, which indicates that one of his main concerns was how his people would relate to the world, that is, to non-Christian society or godless secularism. He indicated that his people had been given to him out of the world (verse 6), but were not to be taken out of it (verse 15); that they were still living in the world (verse 11), but were not to be of the world (verse 14b); that they would be hated by the world (verse 14a), but were nevertheless sent into the world (verse 18). This is the multi-faceted relationship of the church to the world: living in it, not belonging to it, hated by it and sent into it.

Perhaps the best way to grasp this is that, in place of 'withdrawal' and 'conformity', which are wrong attitudes to the world, we see the right one as 'mission'. Indeed, the church's mission in the world is possible only if it avoids these two false tracks. If we withdraw from the world, mission is obviously impossible, since we have lost contact. Equally, if we conform to the world, mission is impossible, since we have lost our cutting edge.

It is particularly striking that, although we live 'in' the world (verse 11), we nevertheless need to be sent 'into' it (verse 18). But that is the case. It is all too possible for Christian people to live in the world without having any share in Christ's mission.

Christ's prayer for his people here is that the Father will 'sanctify' us by his word of truth (verse 17), indeed that we may be 'truly sanctified' like Christ, who sanctified himself for us (verse 19). What kind of sanctification is in mind, we must ask, if it is one in which Christ himself participated? How can the sinless Christ be said to have sanctified himself? The answer is surely that sanctification has two complementary aspects, negative and positive. To be sanctified is to be separated *from* evil in all its forms. This is what we usually think about when the word 'sanctification' is used. But to be sanctified is also to be set apart *for* the particular ministry to which God has called us. It is in this sense that Jesus set himself apart for us, namely to come into the world to seek and to save us. We too have been 'sanctified', or set apart for our mission in the world. In fact, we can be described as 'separated from the world to be of service to the world'.[6]

In verse 18 (as in John 20:21), Jesus draws a deliberate parallel between his mission and ours: 'As you sent me into the world, I have sent them into the world.' In what sense, then, did Jesus intend his mission to be the model of ours? There are substantial differences, of course. His being sent into the world entailed both the incarnation and the atonement, whereas we are not God that we could 'become flesh' or die for sinners. Nevertheless, the fact that we are sent into the world like him will shape our understanding of mission. It tells us that mission involves

- being under the authority of Christ (we are sent, we did not volunteer);

- renouncing privilege, safety, comfort and aloofness, as we actually enter other people's worlds, as he entered ours;
- humbling ourselves to become servants, as he did;[7]
- bearing the pain of being hated by the hostile world into which we are sent (verse 14);
- sharing the good news with people where they are.

Unity (verses 20–26)

Jesus' prophetic eyes now peered into the future beyond the apostolic era. He saw the coming generations of his disciples who would not have seen or heard him in the flesh, as the apostles had done, but who would believe in him through their teaching. 'My prayer is not for them [the apostles] alone. I pray also for those who will believe in me through their message' (verse 20). This means every Christian of every age and place, including us. True, we may have come to believe in Jesus through the witness of our parents, or of a pastor, evangelist, teacher or friend. Yet their witness was a secondary witness, an endorsement from their own experience of the primary witness of the apostles. The apostles were the eyewitnesses, specially chosen by Jesus to be with him, so that they could bear witness to what they had seen and heard. There is only one authentic Christ, the Christ of the apostolic witness, now preserved in the New Testament. All believers since the apostolic age have believed in Jesus 'through their message'.

What, then, does Jesus desire for all his believing people throughout the world and the centuries? There can be no doubt about this because he expresses it three times:

verse 21a: 'that all of them may be one'
verse 22b: 'that they may be one'
verse 23b: 'that they may become perfectly one' (RSV)

These are well-known petitions. What is not so well known or understood is the nature of the unity for which Christ prayed. He stressed two aspects of it.

First, he prayed that his people would enjoy *unity with the apostles*. Consider carefully what is recorded in verses 20–21a: 'My prayer is not for them alone. I pray also for those who will believe in me through their message, that all of them may be one.' We have already seen that Jesus distinguishes between two groups of people: 'these' (the little band of apostles gathered round him) and 'those' (the huge company of all subsequent believers) (RSV and NEB). They are the teachers and the taught. He then prays that 'all of them', which must mean 'these' and 'those' together, 'may be one'. In other words, Jesus' prayer was first and foremost that there might be a historical continuity between the apostles and the post-apostolic church. He prays that the church's faith might not change with the changing years, but remain recognizably the same. He prays that the church of every generation might merit the label 'apostolic' because of its loyalty to the message and mission of the apostles. Christian unity begins, then, as unity with the apostles through the New Testament, which makes their teaching available to us. Without this, church unity would not be distinctively Christian.

Second, Jesus prayed that his people would enjoy *unity with the Father and the Son*. Although the punctuation of verse 21 is disputed, most English versions regard its second clause as beginning a new sentence. We might render it as follows: 'Father, just as you are in me and I am in you, [I pray that they] may also be in us, that the world may believe.' The implications of this petition are staggering. For Jesus prays that the union of his people with God may be comparable to the unity of the Father and the Son in the Godhead. He goes on in verse 23, 'I in them and you in me, that they may become perfectly one' (ESV).

So, then, the Christian unity for which Christ prayed was not primarily unity with each other, but unity with the apostles (a common truth), and unity with the Father and the Son (a common life). The visible, structural unity of the church is a proper goal. Yet it will be pleasing to God only if it is the visible expression of something deeper, namely unity in truth and in life. In our ecumenical concern, therefore, nothing is more important than the quest for more apostolic truth and more divine life through the Holy Spirit. As William Temple put it, 'the way to the union of Christendom does not lie through committee-rooms, though there is a task of formulation to be done there. It lies through personal union with the Lord so deep and real as to be comparable with his union with the Father.'[8]

It is this kind of unity (a shared truth and life) which will bring the world to believe in Jesus (verses 21 and 23). Indeed, the main reason why Jesus prays for the unity of his people is 'in order that' the world may believe in Jesus' divine origin and mission. He prays that all who will in future 'believe' in him (verse 20) may enjoy such unity of truth and life that the world may 'believe' in him too. Thus faith gives birth to faith, and believers multiply.

In the final verses of his prayer (24–26), Jesus looks beyond history to eternity, for it is only in heaven that the unity of his people will be brought to perfection. They will see his glory (verse 24), and the end result of the Son's revelation of the Father will be that they experience for themselves both the same love which the Father has for the Son and the indwelling of the Son himself (verse 26). This ultimate unity, comprehending the Father, the Son and the church in love, is certainly beyond our imagination, but it is not beyond our humble and ardent desire.

Jesus' prayer, then, is much more comprehensive than is commonly realized. It is a prayer for the church's truth ('keep them in your name'), holiness ('keep them from the evil one'), mission ('sanctify them . . . I have sent them into the world') and unity ('that they may be one').

One of the tragedies of the contemporary church is its tendency to atomize this holistic vision of Christ, and to select one or other of

52

his concerns to the exclusion of the rest. But, as Archbishop Michael Ramsey said, 'A movement which concentrates on unity as an isolated concept can mislead the world and mislead us, as indeed would a movement which had the exclusive label of holiness or the exclusive label of truth.'

The major preoccupation of the church in the twentieth century was the search for structural unity, but often without a comparable quest for the truth and the life that constitute authentic unity, and are the means by which it grows.

Others have been preoccupied with truth (doctrinal orthodoxy), sometimes becoming dry, harsh and unloving in the process, forgetting that truth is to be adorned with the beauty of holiness.

Holiness seems of paramount importance to others, that is, the state of the church's interior life. But such people sometimes withdraw into a self-centred piety, forgetting that we have been called out of the world in order to be sent back into it, which is 'mission'.

So mission becomes the obsession of a fourth group. But they sometimes forget that the world will come to believe in Jesus only when his people are one in truth, holiness and love.

Truth, holiness, mission and unity belonged together in the prayer of Jesus, and they need to be kept together in our quest for the church's renewal today. I think we can detect them in the earliest Spirit-filled church in Jerusalem, since we are told in Acts 2:42 and 47 that 'the [people] devoted themselves to the apostles' teaching' (truth), 'to the fellowship' (unity) and 'to the breaking of bread and to prayer' (worship expressing their holiness), while 'the Lord added to their number daily those who were being saved' (mission). It seems to me legitimate also to see the same characteristics in the four traditional 'notes' or 'marks' of the church, according to the Nicene Creed, namely that it is 'one, holy, catholic and apostolic'. For 'catholic' includes the concept of embracing all truth, and 'apostolic' includes the vision of being committed to the apostolic mission.

It is important that we do not separate what God has joined. Instead, we must seek the renewal of the church in all four dimensions simultaneously, so that it faithfully guards the revelation which has once for all been entrusted to it, becomes sanctified and unified by this truth which it preserves, and goes out boldly into the world on its God-given mission of witness and service.

Reflection questions from Tim Chester

1　What difference does it make to know that Christians 'belong to Christ', 'know the Father' and 'live in the world' (from John 17:6–11)? What would happen if we neglected one of these truths?

2　What does it mean to be sent into the world as Jesus was sent into the world (John 17:18)?

3　Stott argues that true Christian unity is with the apostles (a common truth), and unity with the Father and the Son (a common life). So which practical steps could you take to pursue unity?

4　Stott identifies four elements to church renewal: truth, holiness, mission and unity. Can you think of churches or movements which focus on one of these to the neglect of the others?

5　Which of these four elements – truth, holiness, mission and unity – is the strongest in your church? Thank God for his work among you.

6　Which of these four elements – truth, holiness, mission and unity – is the weakest in your church? Which steps could you take to pursue renewal in this area?

4

The church's pastors

It would be difficult to think about the life, mission and renewal of the church without giving thought to its ordained ministers. For it is plain from the New Testament that God has always intended his church to have some form of pastoral oversight. Moreover, the condition of the church in every place depends very largely on the quality of the ministry it receives. As Richard Baxter quaintly put it, 'If God would but reform the ministry, and set them on their duties zealously and faithfully, the people would certainly be reformed. All churches either rise or fall as the ministry doth rise or fall, not in riches or worldly grandeur, but in knowledge, zeal and ability for their work.'[1]

Yet there is a great deal of contemporary confusion about the nature and function of ordained clergy. Are they priests, prophets, pastors, preachers or psychotherapists? Are they administrators, facilitators or social workers? David Hare's award-winning play *Racing Demon* portrays a team of Anglican clergy in South London. Each has a different notion of the purpose of the ordained ministry. To Lionel Espy, the gentle and largely ineffective team rector, 'our job is mainly to learn. From ordinary, working people. We should try to understand and serve them.'[2] 'Mostly, in fact, it's just listening to the anger', and like a punchbag absorbing it.[3] In complete contrast, the young charismatic curate, Tony Ferris, is frighteningly self-confident. 'I have this incredible power,' he claims, which enables him to 'spread confidence' around him, but he does so at the expense of other people.[4] The other characters are more modest in their expectations. The diocesan bishop emphasizes the administration of Holy Communion: 'Finally, that's what you're there for. As a priest you have only one duty. That's to put on a show.'[5] His suffragan, the episcopal diplomat par excellence, sees the heart of his job as 'preventing problems growing into issues'.[6] To Donald Bacon ('Streaky'), who sings tenor, gets drunk and describes himself as 'a happy priest', there are no complications. 'The whole thing's so clear. He's there. In people's happiness.'[7] Harry Henderson, the homosexual clergyman, is a trifle more ambitious. 'There is people as they are. And there is people as they could be. The priest's job is to try and yank the two a little bit closer.'[8] Meanwhile, the sincere, agnostic girl, Frances Parnell, sees the ordained ministry as the 'waste of a human being . . . always to be dreaming'.[9]

Some people, seeing clergy marginalized by secular society, and rejoicing in Paul's vision of every-member ministry, question whether ordained ministers are necessary any longer, and suggest that the church would be in a healthier condition without them. Others react in the opposite way. Whether on theological or pragmatic grounds, they put clergy on a pedestal, or acquiesce when they themselves are put there. Then, when the reins of ministry are entirely in their hands, the almost inevitable consequences are either clerical breakdown or lay frustration, or both.

All down its long history the church has oscillated between these extremes of clericalism (clerical domination of the laity) and anticlericalism (lay disdain for the clergy). Yet the New Testament warns us against both tendencies. To the Corinthians who developed a personality cult of leaders, Paul exclaimed, 'What do you think we are, that you pay such exaggerated deference to us? We are only servants, through whom God worked to bring you to faith.'[10] To others, however, who regarded their leaders with contempt, Paul wrote that they must 'respect' them and 'hold them in the highest regard in love because of their work'.[11] Again, 'Here is a trustworthy saying: whoever aspires to be an overseer desires a noble task.'[12] Or 'to aspire to leadership is an honourable ambition' (NEB).

What, then, is the nature and function of ordained clergy? In general, churches have given two answers, depending on whether they see ministry as directed primarily towards God or towards the church. On the one hand, there is the priestly model, in which the ministry is exercised towards God on behalf of the people. On the other hand, there is the pastoral model, in which the ministry is exercised towards the people on behalf of God.

The priestly model

The Roman Catholic and Orthodox churches see their clergy as priests, especially in relation to their role at the Eucharist. Lutheran and Anglican churches have also traditionally called their clergy 'priests', but for a different reason. At the Council of Trent the Roman Catholic Church affirmed that in the Mass a true and propitiatory sacrifice is offered to God, and that the human priest who offers it represents the Christ who offers himself.[13] The essence of this teaching was endorsed at the Second Vatican Council, which said priests are 'given the power of sacred Order to offer sacrifice'.[14] 'They sacramentally offer the Sacrifice of Christ in a special way when they celebrate Mass.'[15] True, they are said to represent the people of God, as well as representing Christ, when they do this. But the heart of their priesthood is still conceived as offering the Eucharistic sacrifice.

Protestant Christians, who place the authority of Scripture over the traditions of the church, cannot accept this. For the fact remains that the New Testament never calls Christian leaders 'priests' and never refers to the Eucharist as a sacrifice. The Greek word for a sacrificing priest (*hiereus*) occurs many times in the New Testament. There is one reference to a pagan priest,[16] and several references to Jewish priests. The word is also applied to the Lord Jesus, our great high priest, who offered himself once for all as a sacrifice for sins.[17] It is also used of Christian believers who are 'priests of God'.[18] This is 'the priesthood of all believers' on which the Reformers laid much emphasis. Collectively, we are a royal and holy 'priesthood', who offer 'spiritual sacrifices acceptable to God through Jesus Christ'.[19] If we ask what these sacrifices are, they all come under the general heading of the church's worship. They include our bodies,[20] our prayer, praise and penitence,[21] our gifts and good deeds,[22] our life laid down in God's service,[23] and our evangelism by which we present our converts as 'an offering acceptable to God'.[24] These eight sacrifices are offered to God by the whole church in its capacity as a holy priesthood. But not once is priestly language or imagery used of a particular group of Christian leaders who might correspond to the priests of the old covenant.

When we remember that the Levitical priesthood had for centuries been central to Israel's life, and still was in the Palestinian Judaism of Jesus' day, the fact that Christian leaders are never likened to priests must have been deliberate. Charles Hodge, the nineteenth-century theologian, said,

> Every title of honour is lavished upon them [i.e. Christian ministers]. They are called the bishops of souls, pastors, teachers, rulers, governors, the servants or ministers of God; stewards of the divine mysteries; watchmen, heralds, but never priests. As the sacred writers were Jews, to whom nothing was more familiar than the word priest, whose ministers of religion were constantly so denominated, the fact that they never once used the word, or any of its cognates, in reference to the ministers of the gospel . . . is little less than miraculous. It is one of those cases in which the silence of Scripture speaks volumes.[25]

Some Reformed churches, including the Church of England, retained the word 'priest' because the English word 'priest' comes from the word 'presbyter'. It therefore translated the word 'elder' (*presbyteros*) rather than the word 'priest' (*hiereus*). 'Priest' was used because 'presbyter' was not a word in common English currency. At the same time, there is evidence that the Reformers would have preferred the unambiguous word 'presbyter'.[26] For instance, John Calvin complained in the *Institutes* that the Roman bishops created 'not presbyters to lead and feed the people, but priests to perform sacrifices'.[27] In England Richard Hooker, answering the Puritans who criticized the retention of 'priest' in the Prayer Book, expressed a preference for 'presbyter', since 'in truth the word *presbyter* doth seem more fit, and in propriety of speech more agreeable than *priest* with the drift of the whole gospel of Jesus Christ'.[28] Today few people know that 'priest' is a contraction of 'presbyter', and even fewer are able to perform the mental gymnastics of saying 'priest' and thinking 'presbyter'. It would therefore be better for both theological clarity and biblical faithfulness to drop the word 'priest' altogether from our vocabulary. We could then follow the wisdom of the united churches of South India, North India and Pakistan, and refer to the three orders of ordained ministry as 'bishops, presbyters and deacons'.

We need to define the essence of 'priesthood' (according to Scripture), and remember that the Old Testament priests were pastors too. They exercised a dual role. On the one hand, as *priests*, they had a *Godward* ministry: 'Every high priest is selected from among men and is appointed to represent them in matters related to God.'[29] In this capacity it was their privilege to approach, or draw near to, God,[30] to offer sacrifices[31] and to make intercession.[32] On the other hand, as *pastors*, they had a *people-ward* ministry. In this capacity they cared for the people's welfare; they taught them the law;[33] they blessed the people, that is, sought or pronounced God's blessing upon them;[34] and they acted as judges and made decisions.[35]

Since the cross, no more sacrifices for sin can be offered. And so the remaining Godward privileges of the priesthood have, through the work of Christ, been inherited by the whole people of God. We may *all* draw near to God,[36] and 'have confidence to enter the Most

Holy Place by the blood of Jesus'.[37] We are *all* invited to offer the 'spiritual sacrifices' of our worship.[38] And we are *all* to pray for one another. None of these ministries now belongs, as they did in Old Testament days, to a privileged caste, to clergy in distinction from laity. Although this ministry of intercession may be a special responsibility of clergy,[39] it cannot be claimed as a distinctively 'priestly' work which is restricted to them.

In Old Testament days the priests and the prophets complemented one another. Both ministries were representative, but in opposite directions. The priests represented the people to God, especially in offering sacrifices; the prophets were spokesmen of God to the people, especially in uttering oracles. But in the new covenant this double mediatorial ministry is now exercised by Jesus Christ alone. It is through Christ that we come to God; and it is through Christ that God speaks to us. He is the only priest through whom we enjoy access to God, and the only prophet through whom we enjoy the knowledge of God. Human mediators are no longer needed.

So it is the pastoral ministry of the Old Testament priests, their responsibility to care for the spiritual well-being of the people of God, and in particular their teaching role, which have devolved in New Testament days on clergy. Insofar as priests were pastors in the Old Testament, I suppose one could call pastors 'priests' in the New Testament. But pastoral duties do not have anything distinctively priestly about them (except perhaps intercession), and in fact, as we have seen, neither Jesus nor his apostles ever referred to pastoral leaders as priests.

But God does want his church to have pastors. True, the pastoral responsibilities of caring and teaching belong in some degree to all the people of God, since we are called to 'teach and admonish one another' and to 'carry each other's burdens'.[40] Nevertheless, the New Testament assumes that each church will have a group of elders whose main task is to pastor God's flock, especially by feeding, that is teaching, them.[41]

The pastoral model

Since 'pastor' means 'shepherd', and the image comes from a rural context alien to today's urban communities, it is sometimes suggested that we need to find a more appropriate term for the church's leaders. City apartment-dwellers, perched on the ledges of their perpendicular cliffs of glass and concrete, know little about sheep and shepherds. Yet I doubt that most us are ready to jettison the self-portrait of Jesus Christ as the 'good shepherd' who came to seek and save lost sheep. Nor are we likely to stop singing the popular hymns which embody this imagery, such as 'The Lord's My Shepherd, I'll Not Want' and 'The King of Love My Shepherd Is'.

We are told that Jesus was moved with compassion when he saw the crowds, 'because they were harassed and helpless, like sheep without a shepherd'.[42] Shepherdless sheep must still arouse his distress and concern. Ultimately, he is himself their shepherd. But he delegates some of this responsibility to under-shepherds.[43] 'Pastors and teachers' are still among the gifts with which he enriches his church.[44] In fact, all Christian ministry is derived from Christ. His ministry is the prototype. He is the true servant, who came 'not to be served, but to serve'.[45] And now he calls us to follow him in the path of service.[46]

Jesus called himself 'the good shepherd'.[47] Elsewhere in the New Testament he is named 'the Chief Shepherd', 'that great Shepherd of the sheep' and 'the Shepherd and Overseer of your souls'.[48] If, then, pastors are under-shepherds, we will be wise to understudy the good, the great, the chief shepherd. For he both taught and exemplified all the main principles of pastoral ministry. The good pastor, who models his ministry on the good shepherd, has at least seven characteristics.

First, the good shepherd *knows* his sheep. He 'calls his own sheep by name ... I am the good shepherd; I know my sheep and my sheep know me – just as the Father knows me and I know the Father'.[49] The ancient Middle-Eastern shepherd was very different from modern shepherds in other parts of the world. Because Western sheep are mostly reared for meat, they live only a brief life with no personal relationship with the sheep farmer. In Palestine, however, the sheep were kept for their wool, so the shepherd had them in his care for many years. As a result, a relationship of trust and intimacy developed between them. The shepherd could know and call each of them by name.

This was certainly the relationship between Jesus and his disciples. He knew his sheep personally. As in the Old Testament, Yahweh called Abraham, Moses, Samuel and others by name, so Jesus knew and called people personally. When he saw Nathanael approaching and said of him, 'Here truly is an Israelite in whom there is no deceit', Nathanael asked in astonishment, 'How do you know me?'[50] Jesus went on to call Zacchaeus by name to come down from the sycamore-fig tree in which he was hiding. After the ascension, Jesus called Saul of Tarsus by name on the Damascus road.[51] And, although at our own conversion we heard no audible voice, we too can truly say that he called us personally.

So perhaps the first and most basic characteristic of Christ's under-shepherds will be the personal relationship which develops between pastor and people. They are not our clients, constituents, patients or customers. Still less are they names on a register or, worse still, numbers on a database. Instead, they are individual persons, whom we know, and who know us. Moreover, each of them has a 'proper' name, a symbol of his or her unique identity, and genuine pastors make the effort to remember their names. Many years ago I had difficulty in recalling the names of two elderly ladies who came to church every Sunday together. As a result, the best I could do was to greet them as 'you two'. So when the ladies in question began to sign their letters 'U2', you can imagine my embarrassment. 'Greet the friends . . . by name,' John wrote.[52]

The best way to remember people's names is to write them down and pray for them. When Paul told the Thessalonians, 'We always thank God for all of you and continually mention you in our prayers',[53] it sounds as if he had some kind of list. It is, without doubt, the regular mentioning of people's names in prayer which – more surely and quickly than by any other means – fixes them in our mind and memory. To forget somebody's name is, as likely as not, a token of our pastoral prayerlessness.

Jesus also indicated that his relationship with his people would be both reciprocal ('I know my sheep and my sheep know me'[54]) and intimate ('just as the Father knows me and I know the Father'[55]). There was something transparently open and guileless about Jesus. He had nothing to hide. It was a mark of his true friendship, he said, that he made himself known to his disciples.[56] This does not of course mean that pastors have to disclose all their secrets to the congregation. But they should at least be willing for the costly and humbling step of forgoing some of their privacy, and of being known to be frail and vulnerable like everybody else.

Second, the good shepherd *serves* his sheep. 'I am the good shepherd,' Jesus said. 'The good shepherd lays down his life for the sheep.'[57] For Jesus is devoted to their welfare, and his whole life is dominated by their needs. God's chief complaint against Israel's leaders was this: 'Woe to you shepherds of Israel who only take care of themselves! Should not shepherds take care of the flock?'[58] Now sheep are not particularly pleasant animals. We cherish a rather romantic picture of woolly, cuddly lambs. But real sheep have no great concern for their cleanliness, and are afflicted by a variety of nasty pests. Hence the need to plunge them several times a year into powerful chemical solutions. They also have a reputation for being stupid. So there is a good deal of dirty and menial work in shepherding. It includes strengthening the weak ones, healing the sick, binding up the injured and bringing back the strays.[59]

Jesus himself laid down his life for his sheep. He was no hired hand, doing his work for money. He genuinely cared for them, sacrificing himself to serve others. Pastors need this sacrificial, serving love in their ministry today. For, like sheep, human beings can often be 'perverse and foolish'. Some can also be demanding and unappreciative, and we will find it hard to love them. But then we are to remember that they are God's flock, purchased with Christ's blood and entrusted by the Holy Spirit to our care.[60] And if the three persons of the Trinity are committed to their welfare, then surely we must be as well. We need to hear Christ's words to us as Richard Baxter imagined them: 'Did I die for them, and wilt not thou look after them? Were they worth my blood, and are they not worth thy labour? . . . Have I done and suffered so much for their salvation, and was I willing to make thee a co-worker with me, and wilt thou refuse that little that lieth upon thy hands?'[61]

Third, the good shepherd *leads* his sheep. Here is another difference between Eastern and Western shepherds. In the West shepherds seldom, if ever, lead their sheep; they drive them from behind with the use of sheepdogs. Because of the Palestinian shepherd's close relationship with his sheep, however, he is able to walk in front of them, call them, and they will follow him. Chua Wee Hian, a former General Secretary of the International Fellowship of Evangelical Students, tells the story of an Arab guide explaining this tradition to some tourists. Then the tourists 'spotted a man in the distance driving a small flock of sheep with a rather menacing stick'. Was the guide mistaken, then? 'He immediately stopped the bus and rushed off across the fields. A few minutes later he returned, his face beaming. He announced, "I have just spoken to the man. Ladies and gentlemen, he is not the shepherd. He is in fact the butcher!"'[62]

Israel's relationship to Yahweh, and especially their passage across the wilderness, are likened to the movement of sheep following their shepherd: 'Hear us, Shepherd of Israel, you who lead Joseph like a flock.'[63] The godly individual Israelite thought of Yahweh in the same way: 'The LORD is my shepherd, I lack nothing . . . he leads me beside quiet waters.'[64] So Jesus, the good shepherd, took over and developed the same picture: 'The sheep listen to his voice. He calls his own sheep by name and leads them out. When he has brought out all his own, he goes on ahead of them, and his sheep follow him because they know his voice.'[65] The reciprocity is clear. If the good shepherd knows his sheep's names, they in their turn come to know his voice. Christian ears are attuned to the voice of Christ. We develop a certain sensitivity to his mind and will. Gradually we come to know instinctively what would please or displease him. And so we follow where he leads and where he calls.

Something similar is true of Christian pastors. It is our solemn responsibility to lead people in a way that it is safe for them to follow. That is, we have to set them a consistent and reliable example. Jesus introduced into the world a new style of leadership, namely leadership by service and example, not by force. The apostle Peter said, 'Be shepherds of God's flock that is under your care ... not lording it over those entrusted to you, but being examples to the flock.'[66] As a matter of fact, for good or evil, whether we like it or not, people will follow us. It is frightening to think how undiscerning many sheep are. That is why it is essential to lead well, to set a good example, with no gap between our preaching and our practice, so that we will not lead them astray.

Fourth, the good shepherd *feeds* his sheep. 'I am the gate,' Jesus said. 'Whoever enters through me will be saved. They will come in and go out, and find pasture.'[67] The chief concern of shepherds is always that their sheep have enough to eat. Whether they are being kept for wool or meat, their health depends on nutritious pasture. So Jesus himself as the Good Shepherd was pre-eminently a teacher. He fed his disciples with the good food of his instruction.

Pastors today have the same paramount responsibility. The ordained ministry is essentially a ministry of the Word, with the sacraments understood as 'visible words' (as Augustine called them), dramatizing the promises of the gospel. The pastor is primarily a teacher. This is the reason why presbyters must be 'able to teach',[68] and they must 'hold firmly to the trustworthy message as it has been taught, so that [they] can encourage others by sound doctrine and refute those who oppose it'.[69] Pastors must both be loyal to the apostolic teaching and have a gift for teaching it. Whether they are teaching a crowd or congregation, a group or an individual, what distinguishes their pastoral work is that it is always a ministry of the Word.

Nothing is needed more today, in either the tired churches of the West or the vibrant churches of many developing countries, than a faithful and systematic exposition of Scripture from the pulpit. 'Do you love me?' Jesus asked Peter. Then, 'Feed my sheep.'[70] Too many congregations are starving for lack of the 'solid food' of the Word of God.[71] The ultimate goal of our pastoral ministry is 'to present everyone fully mature in Christ',[72] and 'to equip his people for works of service' (better, 'for their work of ministry').[73] It would be hard to imagine a nobler ambition than through our teaching ministry to lead God's people both into maturity and into ministry.

How then do shepherds feed their sheep? Strictly speaking, they do not feed them at all. It is true that if a newborn lamb is sick, the shepherd may take it into his arms and bottle-feed it. But normally the shepherd's way is to lead his sheep to 'good pasture' or 'good grazing land',[74] where they can feed themselves. It is not, I think, far-fetched to see in this a parable of sound pastoral education. Spoon-feeding and bottle-feeding are for babes in Christ. Only pasture-feeding will lead them into maturity in Christ. As the preacher opens up the Scriptures, he invites people into them, in order that they may feed themselves in this rich pasturage.

Fifth, the good shepherd *rules* his sheep, accepting that he has a certain authority over them. I am tempted to omit this dimension, but to do so would lack integrity. Bishop Lesslie Newbigin is right to complain that 'the figure of the good shepherd has been senti-mentalized'.[75] In classical Greek the king was known as the 'shepherd' of his people, and the king-shepherd analogy occurs frequently in the Old Testament. For example, the people reminded David how God had said to him, 'You shall shepherd my people Israel, and you shall become their ruler.'[76] This does not mean that pastors are to be autocratic. Nevertheless, alongside the New Testament's emphasis on the humble service of presbyters, there are also allusions to their leadership role, their being 'over' a local church 'in the Lord'.[77] Congregations need to 'obey' them and 'submit to their authority',[78] although their authority is to be exercised through their ministry of the Word and their example.[79] And it is plain from several New Testament passages that if discipline has to be exercised, it will be done through the local congregation collectively, and not through a single pastor.[80]

Sixth, the good shepherd *guards* his sheep. The sheep's chief enemy in ancient Palestine was the wolf; sheep were defenceless against wolves. If the shepherd was merely a hired hand, he would see the wolf coming and would abandon the sheep. He would run away, leaving the wolf to attack and scatter the flock.[81] Only a good shepherd would risk his own life to defend his sheep.

There is no difficulty in interpreting Jesus' allegory. 'Watch out for false prophets,' he had said in another place. 'They come to you in sheep's clothing, but inwardly they are ferocious wolves.'[82] If the sheep are God's people and the shepherds are their faithful pastors, then the wolves are false teachers and the hired hands are unfaithful pastors who do nothing to protect God's people from error. Sadly, there are still wolves in Christ's flock today, deceivers who deny some of the fundamentals of the historic Christian faith. True pastors will not behave like hired hands and run away. They will stand up to the wolves. It will be a costly task. For shepherds cannot shoo wolves away by shouting at them or waving their arms about. They have to get to grips with them, as young David did with both a lion and a bear.[83] In the same way, pastors need to accept the pain and the danger of close combat with false teachers. Vague denunciations will not be enough. Instead, we have to study their literature, listen to their teaching and wrestle with the issues they are raising in order to counter their arguments effectively in our teaching.

While this is a risky ministry, it is also a necessary and compassionate one. We should never relish controversy. It will always be a distasteful duty. The only reason we engage in it is compassion for the sheep. The hired hand takes to his heels because he 'cares nothing for the sheep'.[84] It is only because a good shepherd does care, and care deeply, for the welfare of the people he serves, that he will stand up to error in the church. Shepherdless sheep are an easy prey to wolves. Must it be said of God's flock today that 'they were scattered because there was no shepherd, and . . . they became food for all the wild animals'?[85] Not if we care enough to 'keep watch over our flock'. It is sometimes said that we must always be positive in our teaching, never negative. But this is not true. Jesus himself denounced false teachers. And the duties of the pastor are not only to teach 'sound doctrine', but also to 'refute those who oppose it'.[86] Feeding the sheep and routing the wolves cannot be separated.

In the seventh place, the good shepherd *seeks* his sheep. 'I have other sheep,' Jesus said, 'that are not of this sheep pen. I must bring them also. They too will listen to my voice, and there shall be one flock and one shepherd.'[87] It is clear that by these 'other sheep' Jesus was referring to Gentile outsiders. Yet he could also say 'I have' them and 'I must bring them' in. We need the same kind of assurance in our evangelism. Wherever we live and work, we may be sure that some of Christ's 'other sheep' are there, that they already belong to him in the purpose of God, and that he is determined to bring them in.

This outreach to people who are alienated and lost is an essential part of the pastor's ministry, even if it belongs even more to lay church members who live and work among outsiders. It is true that we often distinguish between 'evangelists' who seek lost sheep and 'pastors' who nurture those who have been found. Yet their ministries overlap. If Jesus, the Good Shepherd, not only feeds the sheep in his fold, but also seeks those outside it,[88] his under-shepherds who understudy him must do the same. If we evade this responsibility, God will again complain, 'My sheep . . . were scattered over the whole earth, and no one searched or looked for them.'[89] Jesus himself will say to us, 'Did I come down from heaven to earth, to seek and to save that which was lost, and wilt thou not go to the next door or street or village to seek them?'[90] On the other hand, if we do go out to bring people in, then we shall share in the heavenly rejoicing 'over one sinner who repents'.[91]

Here then is the beautiful picture of pastoral ministry which Jesus painted. Wherever there are sheep, whether lost or found, there is a need for pastors to seek and shepherd them. Following the example of the Good Shepherd himself, human pastors will endeavour to know and serve, to lead, feed and rule the sheep of Christ's flock, to guard them from marauding wolves, and to seek them when they have gone astray. And then, however little they may have been honoured on earth, they will receive from the Chief Shepherd, when he appears, 'the crown of glory that will never fade away'.[92]

The pastoral ideal exemplified in Jesus the Good Shepherd, which he wanted leaders to copy, needs to be complemented by two other models which he warned them to avoid.

First, Jesus said there are the secular rulers who 'lord it over' and 'exercise authority over' people. 'Not so with you,' he added emphatically. Leadership in his new community is to be entirely different from leadership in the world. 'Whoever wants to become great among you must be your servant.'[93] As T. W. Manson put it, 'In the kingdom of God service is not a stepping-stone to nobility; it *is* nobility, the only kind of nobility that is recognized.'[94]

Second, Jesus urged his disciples not to imitate the Pharisees. The Pharisees loved both places and titles of honour, for these were signs of the people's servile respect. 'Do not do what they do,' Jesus said. Christian leaders are not to be called 'Father', 'Master' or 'Rabbi'

(Teacher). That is, we are not to adopt towards any human being in the church, or allow anybody to adopt towards us,

- an attitude of helpless dependence, as of a child on his or her father;
- an attitude of slavish obedience, as of a servant to his or her master;
- an attitude of uncritical acquiescence, as of a pupil to his or her teacher.

To do so, Jesus implied, would be both to usurp the prerogatives of the Holy Trinity (God our Father, Jesus our master and the Holy Spirit our teacher) and to disrupt the brotherly-sisterly relationships of the Christian family.[95]

Here are two different contemporary models of leadership, one secular (rulers) and the other religious (Pharisees), which nevertheless shared the same basic characteristic: a hunger for power and prestige. Today the model we are most likely to imitate is that of business management. It too, despite some acceptable parallels, is often more worldly than Christian. We have to beware lest, as the status of pastors in society declines, we seek to compensate for it by demanding greater power and honour in the church. The essential mark of Christian leadership is humility, not authority; servitude, not lordship; and 'the humility and gentleness of Christ'.[96]

Chuck Colson, no stranger to political power before his conversion, says, 'The lure of power can separate the most resolute of Christians from the true nature of Christian leadership, which is service to others. It is difficult to stand on a pedestal and wash the feet of those below.'[97] Again, 'nothing distinguishes the kingdoms of man from the kingdom of God more than their diametrically opposed views of the exercise of power. One seeks to control people, the other to serve people; one promotes self, the other prostrates self; one seeks prestige and position, the other lifts up the lowly and despised.'[98]

Reflection questions from Tim Chester

1 How are church leaders portrayed in popular culture? What are the positive and negative aspects of this portrayal?

2 How well do you know the other members of your congregation? What could you do to get to know more people, or get to know people better?

3 In which ways are you serving your local church? In which ways are you tempted to avoid the cost of serving others?

4 Hebrews 13:17 tells us to submit to our leaders, 'so that their work will be a joy'. How do you ensure the work of leaders is a joy?

5 When have you seen examples of pastors guarding their flock from wolves?

6 What might we learn from secular approaches to leadership? When have you seen worldly models of leadership being applied in the church in damaging ways?

Conclusion
The now and the not yet

I began in the Introduction with the tension between the 'then' (past) and the 'now' (present); I end with another tension, between the 'now' (present) and the 'not yet' (future). These two tensions belong together. For it is in and through Jesus Christ that the past, the present and the future are brought into a creative relationship. Christians live in the present, but do so in thankfulness for the past and in anticipation of the future.

As I conclude this book, I'm going to focus on balanced biblical Christianity. Balance is a rare commodity these days in almost every sphere, not least among us who seek to follow Christ.

One of the things about the devil is that he is a fanatic, and the enemy of all common sense, moderation and balance. One of his favourite pastimes is to tip Christians off balance. If he cannot get us to *deny* Christ, he will get us to *distort* Christ instead. As a result, lopsided Christianity is widespread, in which we overemphasize one aspect of a truth, while underemphasizing another.

A balanced grasp of the now–not-yet tension would be very beneficial for Christian unity, and especially to a greater harmony among evangelical believers. We may agree on the doctrinal and ethical fundamentals of the faith. Yet we seem to be constitutionally prone to quarrelling and dividing, or simply to going our own way and building our own empires.

Kingdom come and coming

Fundamental to New Testament Christianity is the perspective that we are living 'in between times' – between the first and the second comings of Christ, between kingdom come and kingdom coming.

The theological basis for this tension is to be found in Jesus' own teaching about the kingdom of God. Everyone accepts both that the kingdom featured prominently in his teaching and that he announced its coming. Where scholars have disagreed, however, is over the time of its arrival. Has the kingdom already come, because Jesus brought it with him? Or is its coming still in the future, so that we await it expectantly? Or does the truth lie between these positions?

Albert Schweitzer is an example of a scholar who thought that, according to Jesus, the kingdom lay entirely in the future. As an apocalyptic prophet, Jesus taught (mistakenly) that God was about to intervene supernaturally and establish his kingdom. The radical demands he made on his disciples were an 'interim ethic' in the light of the imminent arrival of the kingdom. Schweitzer's position is known as 'thoroughgoing' or 'consistent' eschatology.

At the opposite extreme was C. H. Dodd, with his belief that the coming of the kingdom is wholly in the past (known as 'realized eschatology'). He laid a heavy emphasis on two verses whose verbs are in the perfect tense, namely 'The kingdom of God has arrived'[1] and 'The kingdom of God has come upon you.'[2] Dodd concluded that there is no future coming of the kingdom, and that passages which speak of one were not part of Jesus' own teaching.

In place of these extreme polarities, most scholars have taken a middle position – that Jesus spoke of the kingdom as both a present reality and a future expectation.

Jesus clearly taught that the time of fulfilment had arrived;[3] that 'the strong man' was now bound and disarmed, enabling the plundering of his goods, as was evident from his exorcisms;[4] that the kingdom was already either 'within' or 'among' people,[5] and that it could now be 'entered' or 'received'.[6]

Yet the kingdom was a future expectation as well. It would not be perfected until the last day. So he looked forward to the end, and taught his disciples to do so also. They were to pray 'your kingdom come'[7] and to 'seek' it first,[8] giving priority to its expansion. At times he also referred to the final state of his followers in terms of 'entering' the kingdom[9] or 'receiving' it.[10]

One way in which the Bible expresses the tension between the 'now' and the 'not yet' is in the terminology of the two 'ages'. From the perspective of the Old Testament, history is divided between 'this present age' and 'the last days', namely the kingdom of right-eousness to be introduced by the Messiah.[11] This simple structure of two consecutive ages was decisively changed, however, by the coming of Jesus. For he brought in the new age, and died for us in order to deliver us 'from the present evil age'.[12] As a result, the Father has already 'rescued us from the dominion of darkness and brought us into the kingdom of the Son he loves'.[13] We have even been raised from death and seated with Christ in the heavenly realm.[14]

At the same time, the old age persists. So the two ages overlap. 'The darkness is passing and the true light is already shining.' One day the old age will be terminated (which will be 'the end of the age'),[15] and the new age, which was introduced with Christ's first coming, will be brought about at his second. Meanwhile, the two ages continue, and we are caught in the tension between them. We are summoned not to 'conform to the pattern of this world', but rather to 'be transformed' according to God's will and to live consistently as children of the light.[16]

Nevertheless, the tension remains: we have already *been* saved, yet also we *shall* be saved one day.[17] And we are already God's adopted children, yet we also are waiting for our adoption.[18] Already we have 'crossed over from death to life', yet eternal life is also a future gift.[19] Already Christ is reigning, although his enemies have not yet become his footstool.[20]

Caught between the present and the future, the characteristic stance of Christians is variously described as hoping,[21] waiting,[22] longing,[23] and groaning,[24] as we wait both 'eagerly'[25] and also 'patiently'.[26]

The essence of the interim period between the 'now' and the 'not yet' is the presence of the Holy Spirit in the people of God. On the one hand, the gift of the Spirit is the distinctive blessing of the kingdom of God and the principal sign that the new age has dawned.[27] On the other, because his indwelling is only the beginning of our kingdom inheritance, it is also the guarantee that the rest will one day be ours. The New Testament uses three metaphors to illustrate this. The Holy Spirit is the 'firstfruits', pledging that the full harvest will follow,[28] the 'deposit' or first instalment, pledging that the full payment will be made,[29] and the foretaste, pledging that the full feast will one day be enjoyed.[30]

Here are some examples of the tension between the 'now' and the 'not yet'.

Revelation, holiness and healing

The first example is in *the intellectual sphere*, or the question of *revelation*.

We affirm with joyful confidence that God has revealed himself to human beings, not only in the created universe, in our reason and our conscience, but supremely in his Son Jesus Christ, and in the Bible's witness to him. We dare to say that we know God, because he has himself taken the initiative to draw aside the curtain which would otherwise hide him from us. We rejoice greatly that his Word throws light on our path.[31]

But we do not yet know God as he knows us. Our knowledge is partial because his revelation has been partial. He has revealed everything that he intends to reveal, and which he considers to be for our good, but not everything that there is to reveal. There are many mysteries left, and so 'we live by faith, not by sight'.[32]

We should take our stand alongside those biblical authors who, although they knew themselves to be agents of divine revelation, nevertheless confessed humbly that their knowledge remained limited. Even Moses, 'whom the LORD knew face to face', acknowledged, 'O Sovereign LORD, you have only [RSV] begun to show to your servant your greatness and your strong hand.'[33] Then think of the apostle Paul, who likened his knowledge both to the immature thoughts of a child and to the distorted reflections of a mirror.[34]

So, then, although it is right to glory in the givenness and finality of God's revelation, it is also right to confess our ignorance of many things. We know and we don't know. 'The secret things belong to the LORD our God, but the things revealed belong to us and to our children for ever, that we may follow all the words of this law.'[35] It is very important to maintain this distinction. Speaking personally, I would like to see more boldness in our proclaiming what has been revealed, and more reticence about what has been kept secret. Agreement in plainly revealed truth is necessary for unity, even while we give each other freedom in secondary matters. And the way to recognize these is when Christians who are equally anxious to be submissive to Scripture nevertheless reach different conclusions about them. I am thinking, for example, about controversies over baptism, church government, liturgy and ceremonies, claims about spiritual gifts, and the fulfilment of prophecy.

The second tension is in *the moral sphere*, or the question of *holiness*.

God has already put his Holy Spirit within us, in order to make us holy.[36] The Holy Spirit is actively at work within us, subduing our fallen, selfish human nature and causing his fruit to ripen in our character.[37] Already, we can affirm, he is transforming us into the image of Christ.[38]

But our fallen nature has not been eradicated, for 'the flesh desires what is contrary to the Spirit',[39] so that 'if we claim to be without sin, we deceive ourselves'.[40] We have not yet become completely conformed to God's perfect will, for we do not yet love God with all our being, or our neighbour as ourselves. As Paul put it, we have 'not . . . already become perfect' (GNT), but we 'press on towards the goal', confident that 'he who began a good work in [us] will carry it on to completion until the day of Christ Jesus'.[41]

So, then, we are caught in a painful tension between the 'now' and the 'not yet', between dismay over our continuing failures and the promise of ultimate freedom. On the one hand, we must take God's command, 'Be holy because I . . . am holy',[42] and Jesus' instruction, 'Go, and do not sin again',[43] with the utmost seriousness. On the other hand, we have to acknowledge the reality of indwelling sin alongside the reality of the indwelling Spirit.[44] The sinless perfection we long for continues to elude us.

The third tension between the 'already' and the 'not yet' is to be found in *the physical sphere* or the question of *healing*.

We affirm that the long-promised kingdom of God broke into history with Jesus Christ, who was not content merely to *proclaim* the kingdom, but went on to *demonstrate* its arrival by the extraordinary things he did. His power was especially evident in the human body as he healed the sick, expelled demons and raised the dead.

He also gave authority to both the Twelve and the Seventy to extend his mission in Israel, and to perform miracles. How much wider he intended his authority to go is a matter of dispute. Generally speaking, miracles were 'the signs of a true apostle'.[45] Nevertheless, it would be foolish to attempt to limit or domesticate God. We must allow him his freedom and his sovereignty, and be entirely open to the possibility of physical miracles today.

But God's kingdom has not yet come in its fullness. For 'the kingdom of the world' has not yet 'become the kingdom of our Lord and of his Christ' when 'he will reign for ever and ever'.[46] In particular, our bodies have not yet been redeemed, and nature has not yet been entirely brought under Christ's rule.

So we have to recognize the 'already'–'not-yet' tension in this sphere too. To be sure, we have 'tasted . . . the powers of the coming age',[47] but so far it has been only a taste. Part of our Christian experience is that the resurrection life of Jesus is 'revealed in our mortal body'.[48] At the same time, our bodies remain frail and mortal. To claim perfect health now would be to anticipate our resurrection. The bodily resurrection of Jesus was the pledge, and indeed the beginning, of God's new creation. But God has not yet uttered the decisive word, 'I am making everything new!'[49] Those who dismiss the very possibility of miracles today forget the 'already' of the kingdom, while those who expect them as what has been called 'the normal Christian life' forget that the kingdom is 'not yet'.

Church and society

Fourth, the same tension is experienced in *the ecclesiastical sphere*, or the question of *church discipline*.

Jesus the Messiah is gathering round him a people of his own, a community characterized by the truth, love and holiness to which he has called it. But Christ has not yet presented his bride to himself 'as a radiant church, without stain or wrinkle or any other blemish, but holy and blameless'.[50] On the contrary, her present life and witness are marred by error, discord and sin.

So, then, whenever we think about the church, we need to hold together the ideal and the reality. The church is both committed to truth and prone to error, both united and divided, both pure and impure. Not that we are to accept its failures. We are to cherish the vision of both the doctrinal and ethical purity and the visible unity of the church. We are called to 'fight the good fight of the faith',[51] and to 'make every effort to keep the unity of the Spirit through the bond of peace'.[52] And in pursuit of these things there is a place for discipline in cases of serious heresy or sin.

And yet error and evil are not going to be eradicated completely from the church in this world. They will continue to coexist with truth and goodness. 'Let both grow together until the harvest,' Jesus said in the parable of the wheat and the weeds.[53] Neither the Bible nor church history justifies the use of severe disciplinary measures in an attempt to secure a perfectly pure church in this world.

The fifth area of tension between the 'now' and the 'then', the 'already' and the 'not yet', is *the social sphere*, or the question of *progress*.

We affirm that God is at work in human society. This is partly in his 'common grace', as he gives the world the blessings of family and government, by which evil is restrained and relationships are ordered. And it is also through the members of his redeemed community, who penetrate society like salt and light, making a difference by hindering decay and dispelling darkness.

But God has not yet created the promised 'new heaven and . . . new earth, where righteousness dwells'.[54] There are still 'wars and rumours of wars'.[55] Swords have not yet been beaten into ploughshares and spears into pruning hooks.[56] The nations have not yet renounced war as a method of settling their disputes. Selfishness, cruelty and fear continue.

So, then, although it is right to campaign for social justice and to expect to improve society further, we know that we shall never perfect it. Although we know the transforming power of the gospel and the wholesome effects of Christian salt and light, we also know that evil is ingrained in human nature and human society. Only Christ at his second coming will eradicate evil and enthrone righteousness for ever.

Here, then, are five areas (intellectual, moral, physical, ecclesiastical and social) in which it is vital to preserve the tension between the 'already' and the 'not yet'.

Three types of Christian

There are three distinct types of Christian, according to the extent to which they manage to maintain this biblical balance.

First, there are *the 'already' Christians* who emphasize what God has already given us in Christ. But they give the impression that, in consequence, there are now no mysteries left, no sins that cannot be overcome, no diseases that cannot be healed, and no evils that cannot be eradicated. In short, they seem to believe that perfection is attainable now.

Their motives are blameless. They want to glorify Christ – so they refuse to set limits to what he is able to do. But their optimism can easily degenerate into presumption and end up in disillusion. They forget the 'not yet' of the New Testament, and that perfection awaits the second coming of Christ.

Second, there are *the 'not-yet' Christians* who emphasize the incompleteness for the time being of the work of Christ and look forward to the time when he will complete what he has begun. But they seem to be preoccupied with our human ignorance and failure, the pervasive reign of disease and death, and the impossibility of securing either a pure church or a perfect society.

Their motive is excellent too. If the 'already' Christians want to glorify Christ, the 'not-yet' Christians want to humble sinners. They are determined to be true to the Bible in their emphasis on our human depravity. But their pessimism can easily degenerate into complacency; it can also lead to acceptance of the status quo and to apathy in the face of evil. They forget the 'already' of what Christ has done by his death, resurrection and gift of the Spirit – and of what he can do in our lives, and in church and society, as a result.

Third, there are *the 'already–not-yet' Christians*. They want to give equal weight to the two comings of Jesus. On the one hand, they have great confidence in the 'already', in what God has said and done through Christ. On the other hand, they exhibit a genuine humility before the 'not yet', humility to confess that the world will remain fallen and half-saved until Christ perfects at his second coming what he began at his first.

It is this combination of the 'already' and the 'not yet' which characterizes authentic biblical evangelicalism, and which exemplifies the balance that is so urgently needed today.

Our position as 'contemporary Christians' rests securely on the person of Jesus, whose death and resurrection belong to the 'already' of the past, and whose glorious second coming to the 'not yet' of the future. As we acclaim in faith and triumph:

Christ has died!
Christ is risen!
Christ will come again!

Notes

Preface

1 Revelation 1:8.
2 Hebrews 13:8.

Series introduction: the Contemporary Christian – the then and the now

1 Psalm 119:105; cf. 2 Peter 1:19.
2 Dietrich Bonhoeffer, *Letters and Papers from Prison*, enlarged edn (SCM Press, 1971), p. 279.
3 Matthew 11:19.
4 See Jaroslav Pelikan, *Jesus Through the Centuries* (Yale University Press, 1985), pp. 182–193.
5 2 Corinthians 11:4.
6 2 Timothy 1:15; cf. 4:11, 16.
7 Acts 26:25.
8 Ezekiel 2:6–7.

The Church: introduction

1 Titus 2:14.
2 P. T. Forsyth, *The Work of Christ* (Hodder & Stoughton, 1910), p. 5.
3 J. R. H. Moorman, *A History of the Church of England* (A. & C. Black, 1953), pp. 329, 331.

I Secular challenges to the church

1 Trevor Beeson, *Discretion and Valour* (Collins, 1974), p. 24.
2 From an address by Solzhenitsyn, when accepting the Templeton Prize in London in May 1983.
3 Theodore Roszak, *Where the Wasteland Ends* (1972; Anchor, 1973).

4 Ibid., p. 22.

5 Ibid., p. 66.

6 Ibid., pp. 227–228.

7 Ibid., p. 67.

8 Ibid., p. 70.

9 Ibid., p. xxi.

10 Theodore Roszak, *The Making of a Counter Culture* (Anchor, 1969), p. 235.

11 Carlos Castaneda, *The Teachings of Don Juan* (1968; Penguin, 1970).

12 Margaret Singer, *Cults in Our Midst: The Continuing Fight Against Their Hidden Menace* (Jossey-Bass, rev. edn 2003), p. xvii.

13 *The Economist*, 25 November 1978.

14 Peter L. Berger, *Facing Up to Modernity* (1977; Penguin, 1979), p. 255.

15 David Spangler, *Emergence: The Rebirth of the Sacred* (Dell Publishing, 1984), pp. 12, 41.

16 Augustine, *Confessions*, Bk 1, ch. 1.

17 Isaiah 29:13; Mark 7:6.

18 Genesis 28:16.

19 1 Corinthians 14:24–25.

20 Viktor E. Frankl, *Man's Search for Meaning*, originally published with the title *From Death-Camp to Existentialism* (1959; Washington Square Press, 1963), p. 165.

21 Ibid., p. 154.

22 Ibid., pp. 167, 204.

23 From the chapter 'Rebellion in a Vacuum', which was Arthur Koestler's contribution to the symposium *Protest and Discontent*, ed. Bernard Crick and William Robson (Penguin, 1970), p. 22.

24 Émile Durkheim, *Suicide: A Study in Sociology* (1897; ET, 1952; Routledge & Kegan Paul, 1975), p. 246.

25 Desmond Doig, *Mother Teresa: Her People and Her Work* (Collins, 1976), p. 159.

26 *The Autobiography of Bertrand Russell* (Allen & Unwin, 1967), p. 13.

27 Jack Kroll in *Newsweek*, 24 April 1978.

28 Graham McCann, *Woody Allen: New Yorker* (Polity Press, 1990), p. 222.

29 Ibid., p. 248.

30 Stephen C. Neill, *Christian Faith Today* (Pelican, 1955), p. 174.

2 Evangelism through the local church

1 This chapter was written before Michael Green's mammoth book *Evangelism through the Local Church* (Hodder & Stoughton, 1990) was published and came into my hands. Michael Green is a rare combination of theologian and evangelist, and has had an unusually wide and varied experience of evangelism. With that rollicking, infectious enthusiasm with which he always writes, he divides his theme into four parts: (1) 'Issues for the Church' (the nature, necessity, basis and sphere of evangelism in a multi-faith society), (2) 'The Secular Challenge' (four valuable chapters on apologetics), (3) 'Church-based Evangelism' (evangelistic preaching, personal evangelism, missions and other methods) and (4) 'Practical Appendices' (courses for enquirers, discovery groups for new Christians, the training of teams, the use of drama, leading worship, etc.). Here are nearly 600 pages of guidance – theological, personal and practical – from one whose head, heart and hands are together committed to the evangelistic outreach of the local church.

2 John 4:4–15.

3 Acts 8:26–35.

4 Acts 14:14–18.

5 Acts 17:22–23.

6 1 Peter 2:5, 9.

7 1 Thessalonians 1:5, 6, 8.

8 Alec Vidler, *Essays in Liberality* (SCM Press, 1957), ch. 5.

9 John 17:18; 20:21.

10 Michael Ramsey, *Images Old and New* (SPCK, 1963), p. 14.

11 *The Church for Others* (WCC, Geneva, 1967), pp. 7, 18–19.

12 Richard Wilke, *And Are We Yet Alive?* (Abingdon, 1986).

13 *Faith in the City* (Church House, 1985).

14 Acts 8:35.

15 Romans 1:1, 3.

16 1 Corinthians 15:3–5.

17 A. M. Hunter, *The Unity of the New Testament* (SCM Press, 1943).

18 John Poulton, *A Today Sort of Evangelism* (Lutterworth, 1972), pp. 60–61, 79.

19 E.g. Psalm 115:2.

20 E.g. Psalm 115:4–7.

21 John 1:18 (RSV).

22 John 14:9.

23 Colossians 1:15.

24 1 John 4:12.

25 John 13:35; 17:21.

3 Dimensions of church renewal

1 Charles Ross, *The Inner Sanctuary: An Exposition of John Chapters 13 – 17* (1888; Banner of Truth, 1967), p. 216.

2 1 Timothy 3:15.

3 Ephesians 5:27.

4 Matthew 11:19 = Luke 7:34.

5 Hebrews 7:26.

6 Leon Morris, *The Gospel According to John*, in the New International Commentary on the New Testament (Marshall, Morgan & Scott, 1971), p. 730.

7 Philippians 2:7–8.

8 William Temple, *Readings in St John's Gospel* (first published in two volumes, 1939 and 1940; Macmillan, 1947), p. 327.

4 The church's pastors

1 Richard Baxter, *The Reformed Pastor* (1656; Epworth, 2nd edn, 1950), p. 24.
2 David Hare, *Racing Demon* (Faber & Faber, 1990), p. 3.
3 Ibid., pp. 34–35.
4 Ibid., pp. 75, 97.
5 Ibid., pp. 3–4.
6 Ibid., p. 43.
7 Ibid., p. 63.
8 Ibid., p. 71.
9 Ibid., pp. 66, 69.
10 1 Corinthians 3:5, paraphrased and expanded. Paul deliberately used the neuter 'what' rather than the personal 'who'.
11 1 Thessalonians 5:12–13.
12 1 Timothy 3:1.
13 Session 22, 1562.
14 *Decree on the Priestly Ministry and Life*, 1965, I.2.
15 Ibid., p. I.5.
16 Acts 14:13.
17 E.g. Hebrews 10:12.
18 Revelation 1:6; 5:10; 20:6.
19 1 Peter 2:5, 9.
20 Romans 12:1.
21 Revelation 5:8; Hebrews 13:15; Psalm 51:17.
22 Philippians 4:18; Hebrews 13:16.
23 Philippians 2:17; 2 Timothy 4:6.
24 Romans 15:16.
25 C. H. Hodge, *Systematic Theology* (Thomas Nelson and Sons/ Charles Scribner and Co., 1875), vol. II, p. 467.
26 Norman Sykes, *Old Priest, New Presbyter* (CUP, 1956), p. 43.

27 John Calvin, *Institutes*, IV.v.4.
28 Richard Hooker, *Laws of Ecclesiastical Polity* (1593–1597), Book V.lxxviii.3.
29 Hebrews 5:1.
30 E.g. Exodus 19:22; Leviticus 10:3; 16:2.
31 E.g. Exodus 30:20; Hebrews 8:3–6.
32 E.g. Exodus 28:9–14, 29–30; Joel 2:17.
33 E.g. Leviticus 10:11; Deuteronomy 17:11; 2 Chronicles 15:3; 17:8–9; 35:3; Jeremiah 2:8; Malachi 2: 1, 4–9.
34 E.g. Leviticus 9:22–23; Numbers 6:22–27; Deuteronomy 21:5.
35 E.g. Exodus 28:30; Deuteronomy 21:5.
36 Ephesians 2:18; James 4:8.
37 Hebrews 10:19.
38 E.g. 1 Peter 2:5; Romans 12:1.
39 Acts 6:3–4.
40 E.g. Colossians 3:16; Galatians 6:2.
41 E.g. Acts 14:23; 20:17, 28; 1 Timothy 3:1–2; Titus 1:5–9.
42 Matthew 9:36.
43 Acts 20:28.
44 Ephesians 4:11.
45 Mark 10:45.
46 2 Corinthians 4:5.
47 John 10:11, 14.
48 1 Peter 5:4; Hebrews 13:20; 1 Peter 2:25.
49 John 10:3, 14–15.
50 John 1:47–48.
51 Luke 19:5; Acts 9:4.
52 3 John 14.
53 1 Thessalonians 1:2.
54 John 10:14.
55 John 10:15.
56 E.g. John 14:21; 15:15.
57 John 10:11.

58 Ezekiel 34:2. The New Testament equivalent is Jude 12, which speaks of 'shepherds who feed only themselves'. That is, they use their position to minister to their own ego rather than to the people committed to their care.

59 See Ezekiel 34:4.

60 Acts 20:28.

61 Richard Baxter, *The Reformed Pastor* (1656; Epworth, 1939), pp. 121–122.

62 Chua Wee Hian, *Learning to Lead* (IVP, 1987), p. 35.

63 Psalm 80:1.

64 Psalm 23:1–2.

65 John 10:3–4.

66 1 Peter 5:2–3.

67 John 10:9.

68 1 Timothy 3:2.

69 Titus 1:9.

70 John 21:17.

71 1 Corinthians 3:2; Hebrews 5:12.

72 Colossians 1:28.

73 Ephesians 4:12.

74 Ezekiel 34:14.

75 Lesslie Newbigin, *The Good Shepherd: Meditations on Christian Ministry in Today's World* (Faith Press, 1977), p. 14.

76 2 Samuel 5:2.

77 1 Thessalonians 5:12 (RSV).

78 Hebrews 13:17.

79 Hebrews 13:7.

80 E.g. Matthew 18:15–20; 1 Corinthians 5:4–5, 13.

81 John 10:12–13.

82 Matthew 7:15; cf. Acts 20:29–30.

83 1 Samuel 17:34–35.

84 John 10:13.

85 Ezekiel 34:5.

86 Titus 1:9.

87 John 10:16.

88 Luke 19:10; cf. 15:3–7.

89 Ezekiel 34:6.

90 Richard Baxter, *The Reformed Pastor* (1656; Epworth, 1939), pp. 121–122.

91 Luke 15:7.

92 1 Peter 5:4.

93 Mark 10:42–45.

94 T. W. Manson, *The Church's Ministry* (Hodder & Stoughton, 1948), p. 27.

95 Matthew 23:1–12.

96 2 Corinthians 10:1; cf. 2 Timothy 2:24.

97 Charles W. Colson, *Kingdoms in Conflict: An Insider's Challenging View of Politics, Power, and the Pulpit* (Morrow-Zondervan, 1987), p. 272.

98 Ibid., p. 274.

Conclusion: the now and the not yet

1 Mark 1:15, as he translates *ēngiken*.

2 Matthew 12:28, *ephthasen*.

3 E.g. Mark 1:14; Matthew 13:16–17.

4 Matthew 12:28–29; cf. Luke 10:17–18.

5 Luke 17:20–21.

6 E.g. Mark 10:15.

7 Matthew 6:10.

8 Matthew 6:33.

9 Mark 9:47; cf. Matthew 8:11.

10 Matthew 25:34.

11 E.g. Isaiah 2:2; Matthew 12:32; Mark 10:30.

12 Galatians 1:4.

13 Colossians 1:13; cf. Acts 26:18; 1 Peter 2:9.

14 Ephesians 2:6; Colossians 3:1.

15 E.g. Matthew 13:39; 28:20.

16 Romans 12:2; 13:11–14; 1 Thessalonians 5:4–8.

17 Romans 8:24; 5:9–10; 13:11.

18 Romans 8:15, 23.

19 John 5:24; 11:25–26; Romans 8:10–11.

20 Psalm 110:1; Ephesians 1:22; Hebrews 2:8.

21 Romans 8:24.

22 Philippians 3:20–21; 1 Thessalonians 1:9–10.

23 Romans 8:19.

24 Romans 8:22–23, 26; 2 Corinthians 5:2, 4.

25 Romans 8:23; 1 Corinthians 1:7.

26 Romans 8:25.

27 E.g. Isaiah 32:15; 44:3; Ezekiel 39:29; Joel 2:28; Mark 1:8; Hebrews 6:4–5.

28 Romans 8:23.

29 2 Corinthians 5:5; Ephesians 1:14.

30 Hebrews 6:4–5.

31 Psalm 119:105.

32 2 Corinthians 5:7.

33 Deuteronomy 34:10; cf. Numbers 12:8; Deuteronomy 3:24.

34 1 Corinthians 13:9–12.

35 Deuteronomy 29:29.

36 1 Thessalonians 4:7–8.

37 Galatians 5:16–26.

38 2 Corinthians 3:18.

39 Galatians 5:17.

40 1 John 1:8.

41 Philippians 3:12–14; 1:6.

42 E.g. Leviticus 19:2.

43 John 8:11 (RSV).

44 E.g. Romans 7:17, 20; 8:9, 11.

45 2 Corinthians 12:12 (RSV).

46 Revelation 11:15.

47 Hebrews 6:5.

48 2 Corinthians 4:10–11.

49 Revelation 21:5.

50 Ephesians 5:27; cf. Revelation 21:2.

51 1 Timothy 6:12.

52 Ephesians 4:3.

53 Matthew 13:30.

54 2 Peter 3:13; Revelation 21:1.

55 Mark 13:7.

56 Isaiah 2:4.

Enjoyed this book? Read the rest of the series.

Presenting John Stott's classic volume in five individual parts for today's audiences, the Contemporary Christian series has been sensitively modernized and updated by Tim Chester but retains the original core, clear and crucial Bible teaching.

The Gospel
978 1 78359 928 8

The Disciple
978 1 78359 930 1

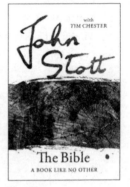

The Bible
978 1 78359 770 3

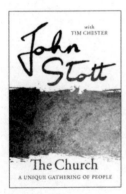

The Church
978 1 78359 924 0

The World
978 1 78359 926 4